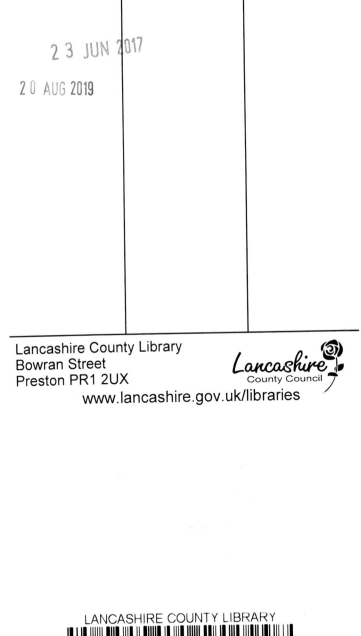

EDDIE
REDMAYNE

EDDIE REDMAYNE

THE BIOGRAPHY

EMILY HERBERT

JOHN BLAKE

Published by John Blake Publishing Ltd,
3 Bramber Court, 2 Bramber Road,
London W14 9PB, England

www.johnblakebooks.com

www.facebook.com/johnblakebooks ⨍
twitter.com/jblakebooks ⨍

This edition published in 2015

ISBN: 978 1 78418 813 9

British Library Cataloguing-in-Publication Data:

A catalogue record for this book is available from the British Library.

Design by www.envydesign.co.uk

Printed in Great Britain by CPI Group (UK) Ltd

1 3 5 7 9 10 8 6 4 2

CONTENTS

CHAPTER ONE: AND THE WINNER IS ...   1

CHAPTER TWO: THE PLAYING FIELDS OF ETON   9

CHAPTER THREE: INTERNATIONAL KLEIN BLUE   29

CHAPTER FOUR: BACKING INTO THE LIMELIGHT   47

CHAPTER FIVE: TAKING RISKS   67

CHAPTER SIX: A ROAD TRIP TO SUCCESS   83

CHAPTER SEVEN: ART FOR ART'S SAKE   101

CHAPTER EIGHT: GOING MEDIEVAL   117

CHAPTER NINE: FROM THE RIDICULOUS   131
    TO THE SUBLIME

CHAPTER TEN: REDMAYNIACS   147

CHAPTER ELEVEN: EMPTY CHAIRS AT EMPTY TABLES   163

CHAPTER TWELVE: I'M AN ASTRONOMER,   179
    NOT AN ASTROLOGER

CHAPTER THIRTEEN: EDDIE IN LOVE   199

CHAPTER FOURTEEN: POTTERING ABOUT   211

CHAPTER FIFTEEN: EDDIE REDMAYNE, OBE   223

SELECTED CREDITS   227

BIBLIOGRAPHY   231

CHAPTER ONE

AND THE WINNER IS ...

February 2015 and Tinseltown had worked itself up into its usual frenetic state brought on by Oscar season: that time of the year when Hollywood crowns its own. Apart from the obvious kudos of winning acclaim from your peers, an Academy Award is a serious boost to any actor's career. Recognition levels, pay levels, the chance of an extended A-list livelihood – these were all on the cards for the Oscar hopefuls and this year was no different from the rest. The Dolby Theatre in Los Angeles was packed to the rafters as first-time host Neil Patrick Harris took to the stage: emotions, as always on this occasion, were running high.

There was particular interest in the Best Actor category in what had been a very strong year. In the running that night were five men: Steve Carell in *Foxcatcher* (as John

Eleuthère), Bradley Cooper in *American Sniper* (as Chris Kyle), Benedict Cumberbatch in *The Imitation Game* (as Alan Turing), Michael Keaton in *Birdman or* (*The Unexpected Virtue of Ignorance*), as Riggan Thomson/Birdman, and Eddie Redmayne in *The Theory of Everything* (as Stephen Hawking). It was a very impressive round-up, containing two of the finest British actors of their generation, and some very popular and successful US stars. Speculation had been mounting as to who would be the recipient of the award: everyone knew that Eddie was a very strong contender, thanks to both the quality of his acting and the intense interest in the story behind the film. He had won worldwide acclaim for his portrayal of the brilliant physicist Professor Stephen Hawking, who had been diagnosed with motor neurone disease at the age of twenty-one and been given just two years to live.

But there were no certainties; no one knew if it would be him.

The moment came when Cate Blanchett, who had actually worked with Eddie some years earlier, ascended to the podium to present the award. She was looking as lovely as ever: she had teamed a simply-cut long black dress with a cutaway detail in the back by John Galliano for Maison Margiela with a statement turquoise necklace made by Tiffany & Co, topped off with an updo for her blonde hair and barely-there make-up. A hush fell over the star-spangled audience. 'And the Oscar goes to …' she began, 'Eddie Redmayne!'

The audience erupted. They bellowed their appreciation,

as Eddie – looking stunned, nervous and absolutely delighted – rose and kissed his wife Hannah before making his way up to the stage where he was greeted with a warm hug by Cate, who looked almost as pleased as he did. 'Thank you,' he repeated over and over, before telling the audience that he was not really capable of articulating his thoughts and adding that he was a 'lucky, lucky man'. 'This Oscar – wow!' he continued to an utterly charmed audience, 'This belongs to all those people around the world battling ALS [amyotrophic lateral sclerosis, or motor neurone disease, the ailment Stephen Hawking suffers from]. It belongs to one exceptional family: Stephen, Jane, Jonathon and the Hawking children, and I will be its custodian. And I will promise you that I will look after him – I will polish him; I will answer his beck and call; I will wait on him hand and foot. But I would not be here were it not for an extraordinary troupe of people.'

And with that he went on to thank everyone he could think of, including his 'staggering partner in crime' – aka his co-star Felicity Jones – before ending by avowing love to his wife. He could not have been more delightful if he had tried and the audience lapped it up. But then, of course, Eddie had attended the greatest charm school in the world, Eton College, and possessed heaps of self-deprecation. To be in his presence was to be captivated by him – you couldn't help yourself. You might as well give up at the first hurdle.

During that appearance on the Dolby Theatre stage, Eddie wasn't just wrapping the bigwigs of Hollywood round his little finger: he was jumping on to a bigger stage still, to what would be the culmination of an astonishing decade that had seen him soar from a total unknown doing bit parts on television to one of the biggest stars in the world. On that night, Eddie joined a small and select brotherhood: A-list British actors. There aren't that many of them but his peers include Benedict Cumberbatch – a friend of his, who was munificent in defeat that year – and fellow old Etonian Damian Lewis. There are a few more, but not many. Eddie had broken into a very select group.

Backstage, he continued to appear stunned and happy, larking about with Cate and paying tribute to the astonishing man who had inspired it all. 'For Stephen Hawking, the illness was of little interest to him,' he said. 'He lives forward, passionately. When I watch a film, I believe what I see on screen. We felt a responsibility to tell their story.' And in a wry aside that reflected he knew how much his status had now changed, he added that at least this would give him some peace of mind about his future career. 'I've always had to fight for jobs,' he confessed. 'Retaining employment will keep me very happy.'

Afterwards, his voice shaking and clearly very emotional, Eddie attempted to sum up what the award meant to him. He explained how even the person who had given him the award, Cate Blanchett, had added to the enjoyment of the evening, as he had previously acted with her in *Elizabeth: The Golden Age*, one of the first films he had ever made. 'She's such an exceptional actor,' he told waiting reporters, using the fashionable parlance of the day, 'so I was recovering from that excitement of seeing her and just trying to bury all this frenzy of nerves and white noise and chimes, and try and speak articulately. And then, of course, you forget everything, but it just felt like an euphoria, an extraordinary euphoria. It's something I will not forget in a hurry.' He also mentioned that he was staying nearby in a hotel with a host of other Brit actors, making the whole thing sound more like a jolly get-together of chums than one of the most important events in the film calendar. Then he started rocking his Oscar as one would a baby and those few people who hadn't been won over earlier were certainly singing his praises at that point.

After the initial shock, he got a chance to relax and enjoy himself, insofar as it was possible for someone whose stock had just taken such a giant leap. There was the Governors Ball in the Ray Dolby Ballroom, followed by the Vanity Fair party, where he was the undisputed star of the evening – no mean feat given the calibre of the others present. Guests feasting on Maine lobster roll, Gruyere cheese gougères with sauce Mornay and In-N-Out burgers included: Joan and Jackie Collins, *Breaking Bad* star Aaron Paul, fellow Brit David Oyelowo, Jay-Z and Beyoncé, Jennifer Lopez, John Travolta, Robert Duvall, Reese Witherspoon and the entire cast of the Oscar ceremony – the sort of crowd with whom Eddie would be mingling from then on.

'I think I've lost it,' he fretted to one journalist who was asking about the whereabouts of the Oscar, but the statuette was located again shortly afterwards and equanimity was restored. The bustle of the party, an annual event hosted by Vanity Fair editor Graydon Carter, took place within the Wallis Annenberg Center for the Performing Arts and was a suitably grandiose affair: a sixty-foot-long copper bar stretched down the room towards a giant mural of the nominees, created by André Carrilho, while women dressed up as cigarette girls in vintage clothing circulated with trays of Cracker Jack caramel popcorn. Cigarettes would have been out of the question, of course. But this was Eddie's world now.

One person, alas, was missing from the proceedings: Professor Stephen Hawking himself. There had been talks about him flying to Los Angeles to attend the Oscar ceremony at least, if not the actual celebrations afterwards, but in the event doctors decided that his health was simply not up to it. Nonetheless, the brilliant scientist was watching the proceedings from across the Atlantic and he made his feelings known shortly afterwards. On his Facebook page – he had joined the site just a few months previously – he wrote, 'Congratulations to Eddie Redmayne for winning an Oscar for playing me in The Theory of Everything Movie. Well done Eddie, I'm very proud of you.'

Others were swift to follow in issuing congratulations. The Liverpool Everyman tweeted congrats to its 'old boy' – a reference to the fact that when he was fresh out of Cambridge University, Eddie had had his second ever professional job at the theatre, appearing in *Master Harold … and the Boys* in 2003 (they printed a picture of an almost unrecognisable

Eddie, too). Everyone seemed to want to claim credit for having discovered him: even Robert De Niro, who had directed him alongside Matt Damon and Angelina Jolie in *The Good Shepherd* in 2006, tweeted, 'Congratulations Ed on your best actor Oscar, it was I that gave you your big break in The Good Shepherd, we all knew!'

Emma Watson, who had starred with Eddie in *My Week with Marilyn*, was next: 'So thrilled for Eddie!' Then came the British Film Institute: 'Congratulations to Eddie Redmayne for winning best actor for his performance in The Theory of Everything.' The Jackie Palmer Stage School, which Eddie had attended as a child, was 'over the moon for Eddie having won the award for Best Actor at the Oscars', as described by its principal, Marylyn Phillips.

Neighbours star Jackie Woodburne, who'd been thanked alongside her on-screen husband Alan Fletcher, was swift to respond: 'Congratulations Eddie on all the accolades for your beautiful performance, and thank you so much for the mention,' she said. 'It means more than I can tell you to all of us at Neighbours, not just myself and Alan. Thank you and good luck with everything you do in the future. Congratulations again.' Alan felt the same: 'To receive such generous praise from an actor of Eddie Redmayne's startling ability and status has been thrilling for both of us,' he explained. And so it went on.

Eddie was pictured beaming as he escorted his wife Hannah through LAX airport on his way back to Britain, the Oscar tucked firmly in his bag. His choice of acting as a profession had been vindicated and then some, his immediate future looking exceedingly bright. So just who was he, this brilliant young actor who had done such a good job in playing the even more brilliant and older scientist? Who was Eddie Redmayne and how had he got to where he was?

CHAPTER TWO

THE PLAYING
FIELDS OF ETON

The year was 1982. Richard and Patricia Redmayne were excited: they were together, awaiting the birth of their second child and Edward John David Redmayne made an appearance early on in the year, on 6 January. Eddie came from what would be considered to be quite a big family by modern standards: in total there were five siblings and half-siblings from his father's two marriages, with Eddie being born to Richard's second wife. His mother had also been previously married, although in her case there had been no children. Eddie's older brother was James and a younger brother, Tom, was also to come along. The family, based in Chelsea in London, was an affluent one, with a very privileged background: Richard was a stockbroker and went on to become the chairman of Cantor Fitzgerald Europe, a leading finance house. This was real upper-middle-class stock, with plenty of money in the background and many decades of professional success.

Eddie's family had been distinguished for generations: his grandfather John was a major in the Army who also went on to work as a stockbroker and Eddie's great-grandfather was Sir Richard Redmayne, a well-known British civil and mining engineer. He worked on the improvement of mine safety and ended up as chief inspector of mines in 1908, the first person to hold the post. Further back on the Redmayne side, the family money originally came from a linen and drapery business based in London's Bond Street in the early nineteenth century. However, for all the prestige and success in his family, there had so far been no involvement in acting. Eddie was about to bring a whole new talent to the family tree.

Eddie grew up in a large house on the Chelsea Embankment, one of the most exclusive areas of London, where houses now go for many millions of pounds, and the family also owned a holiday home in France. There was plenty for everyone to do there – it came complete with tennis courts and a swimming pool, as well as its own vineyard. Meanwhile, back in London, the Royal Court Theatre was near the family home and Eddie became a regular visitor from an early age, although he described having grown up in a house 'that did not have a theatre gene'. But when his talent began to show, his parents were there for him every step along the way.

Patricia (née Burke), the daughter of a customs and

excise officer, ran a relocation business and had a brief early marriage to a Swedish engineer that she met when she was a student at Edinburgh University. After they divorced, she met Richard Redmayne, who was eleven years older than her and also a divorcee. He had two children from his first marriage: Charles, who became CEO of the publishers HarperCollins and Eugenie, who became an investment banker and worked for the Prudential, in both cases having extremely successful careers. Richard and Patricia soon embarked on creating a family of their own. Patricia was a stylish woman, always interested in fashion, and friends recall seeing her shopping in the leading British couture house Catherine Walker – a very exclusive designer much beloved of Princess Diana – accompanied by the young Eddie. She loved to dress him up too and the little boy would often be seen wearing a sailor suit.

Eddie was thus one of five siblings in total, although he was the only member of the family to show any interest in acting. He started when he was barely more than a toddler and his parents encouraged his talent: they sent him to drama lessons and, while still very young, Eddie turned out to be an extremely gifted singer, something that would stand him in very good stead later in life. Although Eddie often attributes both his interest in acting and his talent to his years at senior school, in actual fact it all started when he was so young that it could only have been something he was born with. 'He's a performer and has been ever since he was five and first started singing at school,' his mother once said and, indeed,

Eddie's talent was such that he won a choral scholarship to Colet Court, which he attended in his early years. Colet Court is a preparatory school based in London for the very prestigious St Paul's school (although Eddie did not go there – he was to attend an even more famous school); founded in 1881, it catered for boys aged seven to thirteen.

The young Eddie was a typical student at the school: from a well-off, cultured background (the parents had to be able to afford the school fees), urbane and London-centred. Pupils, who had to take exams aged seven, eight and eleven to get in, were all day boys, that is there were no boarders who would live on the premises. The *Tatler Schools Guide* says of it that it: 'attracts boys who are naturally gifted and hardworking (half-term holidays are cheekily called "remedies"). Colet Court is one of the strongest London preps for games and arguably the best for music. Alongside Westminster it is the top boys' prep in the capital.'

In other words, it was ideal for boys with a theatrical streak and, totally coincidentally as far as Eddie being sent there was concerned, it had some extremely strong links with musical theatre itself. The school could even be said to have played a bit part in its history, with some of the most famous names in musical theatre linked to it. *Joseph and the Amazing Technicolour Dreamcoat* by Andrew Lloyd Webber and Tim Rice was originally commissioned for the orchestra and singers of Colet Court: it had its first ever performance at the Old Assembly Hall of Colet Court in Hammersmith on 1 March 1968 and the second performance, also with

Colet Court boys performing, at Central Hall (Westminster on 12 May 1968), was noticed by *The Sunday Times*. The musical was enlarged upon and a third performance was at St Paul's Cathedral, and since then it has been periodically performed at Colet Court. It had not been planned by the Redmaynes, but Eddie's stage-school lessons, combined with a prep school that had such impressive links to musicals, were providing the foundations for what would one day become an extremely illustrious career.

Eddie is certainly not the only famous pupil to have attended the school, as both thespians and politicians feature heavily in the old boy category: other alumni include Ed Vaizey, Dominic Grieve, George Osborne, Nathaniel Rothschild, Compton Mackenzie and Nicholas Parsons. It was a very privileged environment, one perfect for an artistically inclined individual, and Eddie thrived.

That was not all. His talent for acting and love of the theatre became so evident that his parents, who might not have had any acting talent themselves but were far-sighted enough to recognise that their son did and that it should be encouraged, sent him to the Jackie Palmer Stage School in High Wycombe at the weekends, where he rubbed shoulders with more future stars, including James Corden and Aaron Johnson, who is now married to Sam Taylor-Johnson, the artist who directed *Fifty Shades of Grey*. At every step along the road of his childhood, in fact, Eddie was to encounter people who went on to have some considerable success.

He attended the Jackie Palmer Stage School from the age

of ten, but he kept up the connection even after starting at his senior school. He loved acting and performing, and was thriving as much there as he did at his day school. His teachers remembered him very fondly. 'Eddie applied to join Jackie Palmer Agency when he was ten years old and the moment we met him we knew he was very special,' said Marylyn Phillips, principal of the school, to the *Bucks Free Press*. 'Even when he was at Eton he joined us for the Jackie Palmer Stage School shows at the Wycombe Swan, singing from shows such as *Into the Woods* and *Sweeney Todd*. He couldn't be with us on the stage school's fortieth birthday, due to filming commitments, he still found time to send us a message to say how much he had enjoyed taking part in the shows of such a marvellous school. If you were to ask me what makes Eddie Redmayne so special it is that he has a natural feel whether it is singing or acting. He is at one with the character he is playing; he has respect for the person he is portraying, but above all, he is a very caring, down to earth, humble actor, who happens to be exceptionally talented.'

Attendance at the school bore early fruit: a precocious talent was making itself felt and he made it on to the London stage before he was even in his teens. Eddie's first stage appearance came about when he was only twelve years old, in a West End production of *Oliver!* directed by the famous Sam Mendes, who would go on to direct the James Bond film *Skyfall* to great acclaim. Eddie remembers the experience with typical self-deprecation. 'I was workhouse boy number 40,' he told *The Daily Telegraph*. 'It was such a minor part that I didn't meet Sam Mendes. But his name remained firmly on my CV for a long time.' On another occasion he recalled, 'I had one line: "Books you ordered from the bookseller, sir." I was elated and terrified. That musical was like a rite of passage.' But it showed him that this was the way ahead: 'My lovely godmother took me to the Ivy afterwards and I remember thinking, "Yeah, I can definitely do this,"' he said. It was in fact a breakthrough moment: Eddie has often accredited the exceptional facilities to be found at his senior school, to say nothing of the teaching he encountered there, as setting him on his way, but in actual fact it had all started when he was much younger. Having appeared on a real West End stage and heard the applause (even if it wasn't actually for him), he knew that he wanted to do it again.

Nevertheless, his next school was going to be equally important for encouraging his love of acting, both thanks to the teachers he encountered and the numerous opportunities he had to take part in plays. Most pupils went from Colet Court to St Paul's, but Eddie was destined for possibly the most famous school in the world: Eton College. With fees of £34,500 a year, this was a place that only the most privileged could attend and one of Eddie's fellow classmates was the young Prince William – not exactly a friend, as Eddie put it, but 'a mate'. When Eddie himself became famous, the press was delighted to discover that he'd been rubbing shoulders with royalty from a very young age, but the fact is that in a school like Eton, it would have been unusual not to have been rubbing shoulders with members of the monarchy. Aside from British royals, there were plenty of other very famous people, gathered from all over the world. 'It's the weird thing Eton does – you're at school next to lords and earls and, in my case, Prince William, so you end up being used to dealing with those sorts of people,' said Eddie, revealing that it also gave him an early lesson in handling the press. 'They'd say William was doing something somewhere and I knew he wasn't, because we were both in double French.'

The place had been set up by a king, albeit for boys who were less privileged than the students who currently attend the school, and who needed a helping hand. Eton had initially been founded in 1441 by Henry VI, who also established King's College, Cambridge, in order to provide free education for seventy poor boys. However, by the time Eddie attended, over 600 years later, Eton had come to personify privilege, as the alma mater of nineteen British prime ministers – the rich and famous too numerous to mention – and had been called 'the chief nurse of England's statesmen' in the past.

The very name Eton has connotations all of its own: Old Etonians are said to possess a singular self-confidence of a type that no other school, no matter how excellent, quite manages to impress on its pupils. For some, of course, 'Eton' summons up a class system that is particularly British and by the time Eddie came to prominence, there were grumbles from many quarters that only the over-privileged sent to such excellent schools were able to forge a career in acting. It was nonsense, of course, as there are plenty of talented, working-class actors treading the boards, but it is a sign that even the thespian community is not immune from the class war that still exists in Britain. Another way of looking at it is simply to acknowledge that Eddie attended a very good school.

Eton is now one of just four such single-sex full-boarding schools in the UK (the others are Harrow, Radley and Winchester) and is headed by a Provost and Fellows who appoint the Head Master. Boys are divided between King's Scholars – of whom there are only seventy and who live in the boarding house College – and everyone else, known as Oppidans. This name is derived from the Latin *oppidum*, meaning town, as they live outside the college's original buildings (this came about as the school grew). Eddie was an Oppidan. The school is split into twenty-five houses, where the boys live, each headed by a house master, with a house captain and a house captain of games selected from the pupils, and Eddie attended The Timbralls. The school's traditions have changed extensively over the centuries, but the uniform remains distinctive, consisting of: morning coat (a black tailcoat), false collar, pinstriped trousers and white tie, with some slight variations for some of the senior boys. Teachers, who are called 'beaks', also wear a variation of the school's clothing.

Classes are called 'divisions' or 'divs' and are run across the school, not on a house basis, with classrooms in other buildings. There are many different societies to cater for a variety of interests, including theatre. Past speakers have included Andrew Lloyd Webber, Ralph Fiennes, Rowan

Atkinson and Ian McKellan – clearly an atmosphere in which the artistic could thrive. The school would put on numerous plays every year in one of its three theatres: the Farrer and two smaller studios (the Caccia Studio and Empty Space). In order to facilitate this, Eton hires a Director-in-Residence every year; this is a professional director who puts on one house play and a Lower Boy play, and teaches drama and theatre studies across the school. The department is almost as well-equipped as a small theatre: it has a full-time designer, a carpenter, a manager and a part-time wardrobe mistress.

There are also two magazines, *The Junior Chronicle* and *The Chronicle*, for those interested in showcasing their writing talents. As well as all these opportunities to shine and work hard, pupils have plenty of occasions to enjoy a holiday, such as the Fourth of June (held on the Wednesday before the first weekend of June, whatever the date) to celebrate the birthday of George III, Eton's greatest patron, and St Andrew's Day. On that occasion the boys play the Eton Wall Game, a game which has a slight resemblance to rugby union.

In recent years, Eton has produced a great many of Britain's most successful actors, including Dominic West (who said that in the eyes of the media an Eton education 'is a stigma that is slightly above "paedophile"', but it certainly didn't do him any harm and he subsequently said he would send his own children there), Tom Hiddleston ('People think it's just full of braying toffs … It isn't true … It's actually one of the most broadminded places I've ever been. The reason it's a good school is that it encourages people to find the thing they love and to go for it. They champion the talent of the individual and that's what's special about it.'), Damian Lewis, Edward Woodall, Nicholas Rowe, Oliver Dimsdale, Harry Lloyd, Adetomiwa Edun and numerous others.

Eddie fitted right in and was very popular among his classmates. While not overly sporty, he played rugby at the school in the Rugby Colts (and was heard to profess sympathy for Prince William, on the grounds that everyone wanted to rugby-tackle the future king) but acting remained his main passion. His time at Eton coincided with that of one of the best and most influential teachers/directors of the day, who was to have a profound influence on a whole generation of British actors. For while Eddie was a pupil there, the school's Director of Drama and Head of Theatre Studies was an immensely distinguished man called Simon Dormandy, known to his students as Dormo.

Dormandy, who was also an actor and director in his own right, had a very impressive CV that included work with the Royal Shakespeare Company (where he acted between 1988 and 1995), the international touring company Cheek by Jowl, the Donmar Warehouse, the Old Vic, Chichester Festival Theatre and the Royal Exchange, and he had in the past acted in the films *Little Dorrit* and *Vanity Fair*. He taught at Eton from 1997 to 2012 and Eddie was not the only future star to pass through his hands – others included the aforementioned Tom Hiddleston, Harry Lloyd and Adetomiwa Edun; he also taught the director James Dacre, the comedy duo Totally Tom (Tom Palmer and Tom Stourton) and Humphrey Ker.

There has been a great deal of discussion recently about just how Eton has managed to produce so many excellent actors in recent years and the answer might well lie with Simon Dormandy and his fellow teacher Hailz-Emily Osborne, another extremely talented individual whom the boys in her care could not praise highly enough. Eddie certainly thought the duo were the reason why so many of his peers went on to have such distinguished careers: 'They treated us like professionals and we had a state-of-the-art theatre which meant that the adjustment between school and working professionally didn't feel like that much of a leap,' he told the *Radio Times*. Despite their charges' young age, the duo demanded – and got – astonishing results from their pupils, teaching them skills that would set them up for life.

On other occasions Eddie was more effusive still about a school, and its staff, that clearly served him as well as any actual drama school could. 'The facilities are exceptional, and if you have an interest in anything – art, design, drama, sport, music – that school will support you,' he told *Intelligent Life*. 'The year after I started, a drama teacher arrived called Simon Dormandy, and he treated us like professional actors. He had high expectations – you played women, you played old men, you were pushed outside your comfort zone. Everything you see about Eton from the outside is very structured: it's hierarchy and order, all uniforms and collars.

But Simon encouraged freedom and playfulness and allowed you the room to make mistakes. Most importantly, for me, he taught us how to speak verse. I did "Henry VI" and "Richard III" there, and I suppose that's where it all began.' He took part in plenty of other plays, too, including modern ones such as *Pravda* – the David Hare and Howard Brenton satire on the newspaper industry – *Jesus Christ Superstar*, in which he played Herod, and many more.

Dormandy realised immediately that he was dealing with an outstanding pupil. 'His talent was obvious and innate,' he once said. 'I knew as soon as I met him that he was exceptionally gifted. He was able and happy to be very raw. That remains part of the essence of why he's such an extraordinary actor.'

Eddie thrived in the theatricals at Eton; he appeared in *A Midsummer Night's Dream*, as well as playing, under the auspices of Dormandy, the female role of Adela Quested in *A Passage to India*, something that allowed him to show off the full range of his talents. It wasn't his only female role, either (one of the advantages of a single-sex school is that it enables putative thespians to experiment not only with taking on different parts, but different genders too). Hailz-Emily Osborne was also mightily impressed with her young charge, whom she first saw acting in another woman's role when she visited the school to judge a competition. 'He had been given a non-speaking role as Queen Charlotte in an excerpt of *The Madness of King George*,' she recalled to the *Radio Times*.

'All Eddie had to do was stand and look terribly concerned while the older boy hammed it up and went mad, but I was just riveted by him. He came across as so professional, even at that young age.' She later added, 'I didn't give that play the prize but when I summed up, I said there was an outstanding performer and it was the little boy playing Queen Charlotte who just watched everything that was going on – and that was Eddie.' He clearly had a natural talent, and with two such influential teachers behind him, he received every bit of encouragement and coaching that he needed right from the start.

In later years, when the extent of their own influence was beginning to become clear, both teachers came under a fair bit of scrutiny themselves, given quite how well their alumni were beginning to do. Their protégés were not just doing well in the UK – the likes of Damian Lewis and Dominic West were cleaning up in *Homeland* and *The Wire*, both hard-hitting US television series, where they blended in so well that most of the US viewers didn't realise they weren't actually Americans. As the head of Eton once put it, 'When HBO want a gritty, hard-bitten, authentically American character to head up a mini-series they instinctively think: Old Etonian.'

The reason for their success, according to both of their former teachers, was at least in part due to the rigours of a classical education and an insistence on the highest standards. 'We really don't do a line in floppy hair here,' Hailz-Emily told *The Guardian*, firmly refuting the popular image of what an Old Etonian usually looks like.

Dormandy explained it too. 'Music has always been part of the curriculum. With drama it is different,' he said. 'For me the importance the work has here in the boys' lives is the reason they do such good work afterwards. That importance arises from many things. One is that we don't do drama just for its educational value. We do a play as a work of art, to be explored at its fullest. Another reason is that there's an intensity here because the boys are boarding.' However, they also did push boys into further education, as he explained, 'Although with some boys it is clear they would make a mess of university because they are just so desperate to act.'

As mentioned before, another advantage to learning how to act at Eton was that the lack of girls meant the boys had to take on female parts, as indeed Eddie did, and this made them a lot more versatile. Eddie claimed that this helped him to get his first-ever professional role, and he was so influenced by Simon and so valued his judgement that he continued to ask him for advice well after his professional career had begun.

The enclosed atmosphere was another bonus, as the boys were not made to feel self-conscious about what they were asked to do. In a mixed school, or one where the boys are expected to be macho and streetwise, many might have been afraid of making themselves look foolish, but that was not an issue at Eton. 'Boys don't have to prove themselves on the street, or to girls in the class,' Dormandy explained. 'So you can get them to do preposterous and embarrassing things, such as playing women on stage. The lack of inhibition also surprises people. This place isn't full of boys with silver spoons in their mouths.'

In later years, Eddie was able to look back on it and realise that because the young are so often fearless, he could tackle adult roles that a more experienced actor would have considered quite daunting. And there was a further bonus: Eddie was able to combine learning his future craft with all the advantages of a classical education. 'Between the ages of fourteen and eighteen, I was at Eton, and when I look back on it, it was sort of a massive Shakespeare immersion,' he told *Vogue*. 'I played Henry VI and various other epic roles, which now would be utterly terrifying, but in the greenness of being fourteen, fifteen years old you're like, "Yeah, I can tackle Hamlet. Not a problem."'

But he was well aware, both then and now, that he came from a very privileged background, one which was not granted to everyone and which would set him up for life, whatever path he chose. Contrary to the public image, boys at Eton do not necessarily believe that they are more deserving than the rest of the population; they realise that they are very lucky to be there much more than they are usually given credit for. Eddie was very fortunate to have received such excellent education, but he was well aware of it and never took it for granted. 'I had an incredibly privileged upbringing,' Eddie told *Intelligent Life*. 'When I was working in a pub and going to endless unsuccessful auditions, I could live at home rent-free in London. That was the really great privilege.'

Eton saw him form another relationship that was to become rather important, too. When taking part in a fashion show at another school, he spotted a very pretty girl and decided to make her acquaintance. He discovered she was called Hannah Bagshawe, and when relating the circumstances of their meeting, he uses his typically self-deprecating style. 'I had to walk across the stage topless – I was this pasty, freckly guy and when I came on the girls in the audience didn't take much notice of me, but I was followed by the best-looking boy in the school and all the girls erupted in cheers, which was emotionally scarring,' he said. 'I saw Hannah across the room at a party afterwards and she was very beautiful and very funny and she loves the arts and theatre just as I do, so we became friends.'

The two became indeed close for a while but were parted from one another when they went to different universities – in Hannah's case to Edinburgh and in Eddie's case Cambridge. And whatever Eddie might have said about his physical attributes, he was actually going to go on to develop a sideline in modelling. Even then it was clear that he had the figure and the bone structure which would make him right for the job.

When he was sixteen, Eddie landed his first professional role: he played John Hardy in an episode of CITV's *Animal Ark*, a series based on the books by Lucy Daniels and shown on 19 May 1998. Eddie's character returned home from school for the holidays, only to find that his pub landlord father had got engaged to barmaid Sara three years after his mother's death – something he has neglected to mention to his son. It didn't set the world alight, but it was a start.

In 2000 Eddie became part of the elite of the elite when he was elected to the Eton Society, more commonly known as Pop. This is Eton's oldest and most prestigious society, dating back to 1811 and originally a debating society (Popina is the Latin for 'tea shop'), whose new members are elected by the existing ones. Prince William was also a member of Pop, but David Cameron, the future prime minister, was not. The most notable thing about them to the outside world was that they were allowed to wear their own waistcoats, which resulted in a veritable fashion parade, as each boy sought to become the showiest peacock of them all. (Prince William's waistcoats were always said to be very conservative; Eddie's taste in them remains unknown.) Members of Pop had a room to themselves, which was not overly opulent, and no one was in any doubt that these were the future masters of the world.

'It was a bit like a St James's club in that boys were put up for election but if there was a single blackball against them then they weren't in,' one erstwhile member of Pop told the *Daily Express* in 2011. 'Things have changed more recently and now the Eton masters have a right of veto. You probably don't get quite so many bad eggs. When a boy got elected into Pop we'd all charge round to his house making a lot of noise. His room might be trashed and he'd usually end up in the bath covered in beans, spaghetti, eggs and whatever else we could find in his locker. Pop was predominantly filled with sports buffs and swells and that's still pretty accurate to this day. It appeals to people who like to dress up as a peacock.'

Members of Pop were able to tell the younger boys what to do, although no longer to the extent they had been able to previously, when they had been allowed to administer beatings (known as 'Pop tans'). Also, membership of Pop was considered so prestigious that it quite overshadowed anything else anyone was ever to achieve in the rest of their life.

'One of the strange things about Pop is that it never goes away,' said another ex-member. 'You find it cropping up in a lot of Etonians' obituaries. These are people who may well have won VCs or who are captains of industry – and yet for some reason the fact that they were a member of Pop is seen to be on a par with anything else that they've done.'

Eddie, of course, was going to go on to win almost every award going in his future career and in the unlikely circumstance he might have felt membership of Pop to be the pinnacle of his life to date, he has been sensible enough not to say so. He was certainly beginning to sense what he wanted to do, although to please his parents he went along with some more conventional career routes, including spending some time in his holidays getting some work experience in the world of finance, where his father worked. He didn't take to it. 'It was the greatest feat of acting ever working there,' he said later, 'having to pretend I knew what a share was when I didn't have a clue.' A career in finance, chosen by so many other members of his family, was clearly not an option.

And so his time at Eton came to an end. The next stage in his development awaited – but what would it be?

CHAPTER THREE

INTERNATIONAL KLEIN BLUE

If Eton is the grandest school in the world, then Trinity College, Cambridge, is one of the grandest colleges in any university anywhere. The University of Cambridge is divided into thirty-one colleges: while subjects are taught in faculties across the campus, students apply to particular colleges and live in them for all or part of their time at the university. The faculties lay on lectures at central lecture theatres, which all students attend, and they may also have tutors in other colleges, but for a great deal of the time they are based in their own college. And Eddie picked the richest, the most famous, the most notorious (it had links with the 1950s spies) and the most extraordinary of them all in which to spend his university years.

Trinity College nestles at the end of Trinity Street in the

very heart of Britain's most beautiful university city. On one side of it is Gonville and Caius College and on the other is St John's – all enormous institutions in their own right – and Trinity is the biggest of them all. It was founded in 1546 by Henry VIII and is the largest college in Oxbridge: thirty-two members of Trinity have won Nobel prizes out of Cambridge's total of ninety. British university members have won six Fields Medals in mathematics (one of the highest honours a mathematician can achieve): Trinity accounted for five of them. Like Eton, veritable hordes of the great and the good have passed through its doors, including six prime ministers, the physicists Isaac Newton and Niels Bohr, and the philosophers Ludwig Wittgenstein and Bertrand Russell.

It has been home to royalty – Edward II, George VI and more recently Prince Charles – and spies, such as Kim Philby, Guy Burgess and Anthony Blunt. It has numerous societies, including the Trinity Mathematical Society, the oldest of its kind in the UK. It has also provided several members of the Apostles, an intellectual secret society that was founded in 1820. It is the richest Oxbridge college and one of the biggest landholders in the UK, as its landholdings alone are worth £800 million. All sorts of stories circulate about its history; for example, Lord Byron was supposed to have kept a pet bear in the college.

Trinity is a stunning building, in a city where there are a fair few impressive buildings to choose from. It is centred around Great Court, designed by Thomas Nevile and built between 1599 and 1608, although its oldest surviving buildings are King's Hostel (constructed 1377–1416) and the site of an earlier college, now defunct, called King's Hall. Other prominent parts of the college include Nevile's Court, built in 1614, which houses the Wren Library, designed by Sir Christopher Wren and completed in 1695. It is one of the best libraries in Cambridge, owning among much else two of Shakespeare's First Folios, a fourteenth-century manuscript of *The Vision of Piers Plowman* and letters written by Sir Isaac Newton.

Elsewhere, there is the sixteenth-century Trinity College Chapel; Bishop's Hostel, which dates from 1671 and was designed by Robert Minchin; New Court, which dates from 1825 and was built by William Wilkins; Whewell's Court across the street dating from 1860 and 1868 (there are two of them) constructed by Anthony Salvin; and the much newer Angel Court, Wolfson Building, Blue Boar Court and Burrell's Field, all away from the main and ancient body of the college. Behind the college, the gardens and grounds of the colleges built on the river, known as Backs, flow down to the River Cam. In other words, it was beautiful, idyllic, historic and one of the greatest seats of learning anywhere in the world.

This was to be Eddie's home for the next few years. By this time, certain that a career in acting was what he wanted, he would have preferred to go to drama school, but his parents were not happy with the idea and so to appease them he went up to Trinity in 2000 to read History of Art (an interesting choice, given that he is colour-blind). He was a Choral

Scholar, moving from an alto at Eton to a tenor voice at Cambridge, which essentially meant that as well as studying for his degree, he was expected to sing at the three services of Choral Evensong that took place every week, as well as for special services. The Trinity Choir is a famous one: it has made recordings, performed concerts and toured the world. Eddie was ultimately to decide that he wanted to be an actor rather than a singer, but this was a training that would stand him in very good stead. It also carried with it numerous other privileges, including three free dinners a week in Hall and six annual feasts, along with singing lessons and the costs of any tours catered for. It was a prestigious position in a prestigious place. But Eddie did not just concentrate on classical music: he was also in a band called Blue Tonic, whose name was possibly influenced by his fascination with the work of Yves Klein. It does seem that he might have toyed briefly with moving in that direction professionally, although years later, when a newspaper unearthed a picture of him in the band, he was horrified. 'I don't think anyone will take me seriously now,' he lamented. 'I was a wannabe who sounded like Kermit the Frog.' He was probably being a little too hard on himself – but a boyband was not the direction in which his future lay.

Eddie did not confine himself to singing and he took full advantage of all the many theatrical opportunities that Cambridge had to offer, acting in at least one play every term. There was a whole generation of stars in the making there; also at Cambridge at the time were Rebecca Hall,

Tom Hiddleston and Dan Stevens, all of whom went on to have big theatrical – or film – careers of their own. These bright young students were there primarily to focus on their degrees, but they found, as so many had before them, that the opportunities open to them were overwhelming. Cambridge has turned out huge numbers of actors over the years, so as Eddie was to go to university rather than acting school, he could scarcely have chosen a better one.

Self-deprecation is the name of the game, though, and it doesn't do to show off. Eddie was modest about his intellectual abilities, telling one interviewer he was 'fair to middling? But I have to work hard at it'. He took to the student life with gusto and as well as working hard, he played hard too, with one contemporary remembering that he 'wasn't adverse' to downing four pints in the course of an afternoon.

And exactly as had been the case at Eton, a beautiful historical backdrop played host to the utmost in modernity. Although the city centre dates back to medieval times, the university, at its centre, can boast state-of-the-art facilities in every subject you care to mention, and a Science Park.

Students would cycle everywhere along the cobbled streets, as Eddie was to be pictured doing in later years in *The Theory of Everything*; they hung out in their own colleges but also visited the others, most with great courtyards dominated by buildings around the side. It was nothing new to someone from a background like Eddie's – Eton had actually doubled as Trinity College in the film *Chariots of Fire*. The city is littered with tea shops, including Auntie's, a perennial favourite on Market Square, just off King's Parade, where the students would take afternoon teas.

The colleges have Wi-Fi these days, and all the modern facilities any university would need, but the old traditions live on. Most of the time students dress casually and eat in the college cafeterias (known as butteries) or cook for themselves, but when they attend Formal Hall – the big formal dinners held in the colleges' grand dining halls – they still wear their black student gowns and, in many cases, formal dress. Prayers are said in both Latin and English, and Trinity is famous for the quality of its wine cellar. Many entertain at other times in their rooms, or 'sets', and most colleges still have 'bedders', a sort of matron-cum-cleaning lady, who will clean the students' rooms and make sure all is shipshape.

Many of the famous colleges, including Trinity, are built on the bank of the river and in the spring and summer months, students take to the punts. It's a common sight to see the punter, the person who propels the flat-bottomed boats with a long pole standing at the back, gliding serenely up the river to admire King's College Chapel and the Bridge of Sighs to name but a few of the exceptionally beautiful places to be found along the Cam. Sometimes they would go out of Cambridge, up to Granchester, where the poet Rupert Brooke hailed from. But this can only be done when the weather is right for it. In the winter, Cambridge, in the middle of flat East Anglia, can be perishing cold. The wind comes straight across the ocean from Siberia, around two thousand miles away, and there are no hills or mountains to break it up.

When autumn arrives, the sky turns a particularly beautiful shade of blue in the late afternoon, with the great buildings along King's Parade and Trinity Street silhouetted against it. As it gets colder, the snows come and riding a bicycle in those conditions can be difficult, but still the majority of students manage to get by.

Then in the summer season the atmosphere becomes frenzied, as exams approach, followed by the May Balls, which are in fact held in June. Cambridge can be an intense place and never more so than when exam time approaches: colleges lock their towers, just in case any students should feel a moment of desperation and decide to harm themselves. It is a rare occurrence, but it still takes place and the bedders perform a valuable role in keeping an eye on the potentially overwrought. Students work late in the night, some at the multitude of libraries throughout the city, some in their own rooms or sets. The atmosphere is fevered.

But there is a complete let-up in the tension after exams are over and the May Ball season begins. Most colleges host these all-night affairs in the grounds, and Trinity hosts one of the biggest and grandest: the women wear full-length ballgowns and the men don black ties to enjoy a sumptuous dinner in Trinity Great Court, followed by a night of dancing and entertainment, often with firework displays. A survivors' breakfast is served around 6 a.m., when the revellers can be found, exhausted but happy, tucking into a full English, the cares of the past year behind them. The bridges along the river are lit up and as morning dawns, many will take to the punts, which often play a big part in the proceedings, sometimes acting as a site where drinks are served. The very grandest balls are more formal still, with the men dressed in white tie.

It is common for students to attend not only their own college's May Ball but also others, either by buying more expensive tickets or by 'crashing' – a highly popular pastime among students, who try to get into the balls without the authorities noticing. Of course, the colleges are all well-aware of this and vigilant but many still manage to make their way in. This time of year is also a great one for summer parties in the grounds of the colleges: student mantlepieces will fill up with formal invitations to lunch parties, drinks parties, Pimms parties and all manner of entertainment. Plays are performed throughout the year, but summer sees a particular surge, with the famous Cambridge Footlights holding its annual review, the ADC Theatre – the university's main theatre – holding major student productions and the colleges seeing more plays staged in their grounds.

At the end of it all, of course, is the degree ceremony, which takes place in Senate House on King's Parade. Graduating students walk there from their college, four abreast, in an order that is set out for the thirty-one colleges: Trinity is the second to go (after King's). Wearing their undergraduate gowns and a collar that signifies the degree they are about to receive, once inside, the students are led, one by one, by their right hand to the Vice Chancellor, who gives them their degree: the new graduate rises, bows and leaves. Families are allowed in to watch the proceedings, and afterwards excited groups of graduates and their nearest and dearest assemble on the lawns, many with private celebrations awaiting them.

All that, of course, was still to come for him when Eddie first went up there in 2000. There is a divide between the arts and the sciences at Cambridge: the latter demand a much more rigorous attendance at lectures, while the former are a little more casual. Students could take it upon themselves to decide how many lectures they wanted to attend and most, Eddie included, tended to focus on what interested them the most, avoiding everything else. His attitude was typical and it still meant he had to do a great deal of hard work – it was just a different style of studying.

Eddie, like most arts students, was aware that he didn't have to spend all of his time at lectures in the way a scientist did. 'I always felt a guilt, because the engineering faculty is next to art history, so we'd walk down Fitzwilliam Street alongside these engineers, and their working hours were so long, while all these bohemian-looking people were floating in for a couple of hours' lectures a week and going off to write about, say, Marxist art theory,' he told *Intelligent Life*. 'And then we all leave university with a number, a degree, which doesn't reflect the vastly different amount of hours that go into it.' That was a little disingenuous – arts students still had to do a lot, but in Eddie's world self-deprecation is all.

In any case, he was passionately interested in his subject, expounding on it at some considerable length in later years. 'Well, I specialized in late-nineteenth-century/early-twentieth-century French and British art, but then I wrote my dissertation on Yves Klein, who created the color International Klein Blue, which I became obsessed with,' he told *Vogue* magazine at the time, when he was performing in a play about the artist Mark Rothko. In fact that obsession with blue was to become something of a trademark with Eddie, with him even wearing a blue suit to the Oscars.

He went on to say: 'A lot of the Rothko stuff here, like his obsession with the luminescence of his paintings and finding just the right red, sort of feeds into what Klein was doing. When you paint a canvas, there's a luminous quality to the paint when it's wet, and when it dries it darkens and loses any of that iridescence and that life. And so Klein scientifically created this color, IKB, in which the pigment retains that vibrancy. It sounds pretentious and ridiculous when I talk about it, but when I put someone in front of one of his canvases, they go, "Oh, I get it" because it has such an overwhelming impact. Klein was also so theatrical. He put on those amazing Happenings. There was this one in Paris, where he composed the monotone thing and the naked women were painted blue. The elite of Paris society was there, dressed in white tie, and they were given blue cocktails as they came in. And the next morning, they got a big surprise when they discovered that their urine was blue – or so the myth goes.' Those were hardly the words of someone coasting along at university and doing nothing – Eddie was clearly passionately interested in his subject.

The nearby Fitzwilliam Museum was one place where he could go to find inspiration and, of course, all Cambridge colleges – especially Trinity – were bursting at the seams with great art.

Eddie threw himself into every aspect of his life in Cambridge and in the summer he did what so many undergraduates do: he went to perform at the Edinburgh Festival. He participated in a production of *Cabaret* at the Underbelly in the Cowgate, fetchingly dressed in fishnets and PVC. It was put on by a production company called Doubled Edge Drama, which was connected to Eton. *Cabaret*, best known as the film starring Liza Minnelli, was set in Berlin at the time of the Weimar Republic; Eddie, then nineteen, played the part of Emcee – the figure who presides over the drama as it is unfolding – with gusto. His parents saw him in the role and it was later claimed that this was when they knew that their son had it in him to be an actor.

And Eddie certainly felt that this had been an important moment in his fledgling career, as he later said that the 'grotty, grimy venue' was where he 'really got the bug' for acting. However, Eddie credited quite a few different places with giving him the bug for acting, depending on who he was talking to (Old Etonians are not known for their charm for nothing). Whatever is the case, his whole family was thrilled, not just his parents. Eddie's maternal grandmother, Mary Burke, saw her grandson in the role and was impressed. 'It wasn't so much that we could see he was a promising actor, just that he was an actor, simple as that,' she told *The*

Scotsman. 'He was always performing, even as a young boy.'

And Ed Bartlam, director of Underbelly, was also extremely impressed. 'It was our second year at Underbelly so we were very much finding our feet and it was all very atmospheric,' he said. 'Eddie was a slightly creepy Master of Ceremonies in the show and would come up behind people's backs in the audience and get a fantastic reaction. He had left Eton by then and this was one of his first performances and I'm sure his first Fringe performance. I still remember it as one of the best shows we ever did.'

It was while he was in his second year at Cambridge that Eddie got his first really big break. In February 2002 the Globe Theatre was planning on staging an all-male production of Shakespeare's *Twelfth Night* (as indeed it would have been performed in the Bard's day, when women did not take to the stage) at Middle Temple Hall, starring Mark Rylance, and they were casting around for the right man to play the heroine, Viola. They asked Eddie's old teacher/director at Eton, Simon Dormandy for a recommendation and he referred them to Eddie, who had been, after all, cast in female roles before. He had the right looks for it – even now, a man in his thirties, he has a delicacy to his appearance which means female roles suit him well.

Twelfth Night is a comedy about mistaken identity: Viola is washed up in Illyria on the back of a shipwreck and believes her twin brother to be dead so she disguises herself as a boy, Cesario, and goes to work for Duke Orsino. The latter, who thinks Viola/Cesario is a man, sends her to court Olivia on his behalf. But Viola falls in love with Orsino and Olivia falls in love with Cesario – a convoluted situation even for Shakespeare's cross-dressing comedies, not least because a male actor was playing a woman who disguises herself as a man. Usually these days, of course, Viola is played by a woman, stripping out one layer of the complexity, but this was how it was done originally and Eddie was given a chance to shine.

This staging was to commemorate the 400th anniversary of the occasion when Shakespeare's players left their theatre, the Globe, on the south side of the river Thames and came across to the north side, where they performed for the lawyers of Middle Temple. Eddie auditioned and was called back by the play's director Tim Carroll; it was, 'when I was well into a bottle of wine with a friend in Notting Hill. I had to go straight to the Globe and do a scene with Mark who I think was in a rehearsal dress,' said Eddie. But he got the gig and held his own against the great Mark Rylance, widely considered to be something of a coup in itself.

Cambridge gave him an official reprieve to do the play and so in order to keep up with his studies, Eddie would perform by night and then work in the Courtauld Institute library, which was nearby. Therefore, that term was spent both studying for a degree and further developing his stagecraft. 'I was given this amazing opportunity to learn voice and verse, to a certain extent, but with a work in progress and some of the best people in the world,' he told the *Official London Theatre Guide*. 'And certainly from Mark I learnt a lot about invention, more than anything else, and having the balls to be free.'

This was a huge leap forward for Eddie and provided the momentum for a huge future career – and probably alleviated the need to go to drama school. What would be the point when he had already embarked upon his career? Tim Carroll was directing the play and described Eddie as 'quite troublingly beautiful'. The critics seemed to agree and one wrote that Eddie was 'scandalously persuasive as Viola' and 'would bring out the bisexual in any man'. Although he had another year left to go at Cambridge – which he completed – scores of agents took note of the performance, realising even at that early stage that they had a major new talent in their midst.

The production was to be staged over and over again and when it went to New York some years later, Rylance, who was playing the role of Olivia, remembered how it had all come about. 'This production was created for the 400th anniversary of the first recorded version of *Twelfth Night*, in 1602, which took place at a hall that still stands in London called the Middle Temple Hall,' he told New York's *Time Out*. 'We were invited to create an original-practices production of *Twelfth Night* there. This was maybe our fourth or fifth attempt at all-male original practices. As artistic director at that time, I actually wanted to play the fool, Feste. But we realized that we were going to need some very young boys – Eddie Redmayne was actually the first boy to play Viola, and he was not yet a professional actor; he was still in the equivalent to an English high school [sic] – and we felt that it would be better for me to be among the boys playing girls, because I had a little bit more experience.'

To hold one's own at this level so early on in a career is noteworthy indeed and Eddie could have been forgiven for doing as others have done in the past and dropping out of his last year at university. But he didn't: he went back and completed his degree. However, this early success undoubtedly contributed to his growing conviction that acting was the path he wanted to take. It certainly wasn't unheard of for students to take an active part in the world of theatre before they graduated – when the comedian Peter Cook was at Cambridge, he was writing sketches for the review show *Pieces of Eight* – but even so, it marked Eddie out as the coming man. Great things lay in store.

And so it was back to the city of cobblestones and May Balls, swotting for exams and enjoying lazy afternoons by the river – the place once wittily dubbed as that of 'perspiring dreams' in response to the description of Oxford as a city of 'dreaming spires' – the world-class university where Eddie was earning his degree and studying the crafts of his trade.

But it wasn't all work and acting; there was time for romance, too. Hannah was far away in Edinburgh and therefore out of the picture for the moment, but Eddie had met someone else. That someone else was his fellow student Tara Hacking, with whom he had his first long-term relationship. This one also had roots in the past: the pair had known one another since Eddie was fourteen.

He managed his exams, despite his colour blindness, which he described in a later interview with the *Official London Theatre Guide*: 'In your exams you would have these envelopes with images in them,' he said. 'I remember there was one about chalk drawings, the difference between black chalk and red chalk; I had no idea! ... For me colour blindness feels like you haven't really been taught colours particularly well so a dark blue I'll think is a purple and a purple with lots of whites in it I'll think is a blue. Particular tones of green and brown and red become confusing.'

In 2003, Eddie graduated with a 2:1 – a very respectable degree – and made his way out into the world, achieving almost instant success. But funnily enough, it was on a sort of return to Cambridge that he won his Oscar (becoming the ninth Cambridge man to do so) and achieved worldwide recognition. He was catapulted to the top of the A-list by playing another of the city's most famous sons: Professor Stephen Hawking. 'I'd been at Cambridge so I'd seen Stephen at a distance and knew that he studied black holes, but I'd been studying Renaissance paintings,' he told *Wired*.

His time at the university had given him an insight into how to portray genius. 'Everyone was like, "How are you going to play that extraordinary brain?!" I just didn't sleep for months thinking about that,' he described. 'Then I had this epiphany: When I was at Cambridge I met some pretty bright people, and the one thing that I took from it was that people who are seriously fucking bright don't show it. They have no need to. They're so confident in their intellect that they don't tell you.'

And so the wheel came full circle: one Cambridge man played another very famous Cambridge man and became very famous himself in the process. Eddie had studied at the university and while not in the same intellectual league as the likes of Hawking – very few people are – absorbed enough of the environment to know how to play him. It was a difficult role, but then Eddie was not one to shy away from difficult roles, making some very challenging career choices that would have been beyond the reach of a lesser actor.

That last summer as a student in Cambridge was the end of the most carefree part of his life. From then on, now that he had graduated amid a blitz of high hopes and congratulations, Eddie would have to go out to make his way in the world, carve out a career for himself in an extremely tough industry and make a name in a competitive environment. His life had been a gilded one until that point and, by his own admission, he still enjoyed all the benefits that a wealthy background and supportive family could bring, but it was time to make his own mark and fulfill his considerable potential as an actor. It was a challenge to which he was to rise spectacularly well.

CHAPTER FOUR

BACKING INTO THE LIMELIGHT

Eddie has always admitted that he has led something of a charmed life and what happened after leaving Cambridge was something of a case in point. He knew that, as he wanted to be an actor, it would be best to be based in London, where the industry was centred. However, for most aspiring actors this would have created all manner of problems in terms of where to live and how to support themselves as they set out on the gruelling round of auditions. In Eddie's case there was no need to worry: he simply moved back in with his parents.

It didn't take long for his career to get underway, but he was later to confess to enormous insecurity at the beginning of it all. This is very common for all actors – it is a notoriously unstable profession – but in his case was exacerbated by the lack of formal training at drama school. 'I didn't go to drama school, so there was no official transformation stage, no moment where I got a certificate, even a bit of paper, saying "right, you're allowed to do this now,"' he said in an interview in *The Independent*. 'After university, I gave myself a year. I was working in a pub and doing excruciating auditions and wondering if my new agent who'd taken this huge punt on me would sack me, and I remember getting a part in an episode of *Doctors* and it was probably the most exciting thing that had ever happened in my life. Then I went to Liverpool to do a play called *Master Harold ... and the Boys* and I was living in a hostel on my own for three months and it was the most wonderful experience. I started to think, secretly, "well, maybe I can do this". But I came back to London and nobody took any notice and I went back to work at the pub. I always felt a bit fraudulent, like I was waiting to be exposed.' Again, this is not an uncommon feeling at all, but Eddie was shortly to embark on not one, but two successful careers.

That appearance on *Doctors* was actually Eddie's second foray into television, as his first had come in *Animal Ark* while he was still at school. The programme, which has been running since 2000, revolves around the lives of the people who work in a Birmingham medical practice and Eddie's episode, in which he played a character called Rob Huntley, was called 'Crescendo' and was broadcast on 17 December 2003. After he became famous it duly turned up on YouTube.

It makes for interesting viewing. The episode actually

opens with Eddie, in his bedroom, wearing a school uniform and looking about fifteen (he was actually supposed to be seventeen), as he was being bullied by an overbearing father who wants him to become an RAF pilot like he used to be. Instead of going to school, however, Rob sneaks off to the doctor, where it is revealed that his mother was a famous concert pianist but that the pair are no longer in touch. Moments later said mother turns up, explaining why she left – the father didn't want her to have a career and tried to stop her – and it turns out that the father has been hiding the letters she wrote. There is a confrontation between father and son, before the former, who is suffering from angina, collapses. It turns out that the father was trying to stop Rob from becoming a musician too and Rob had faked a urine sample to make it look as though he had diabetes and thus unable to join the RAF.

This was the first in a very long line of roles playing troubled sons and although no one could have said it set the world on fire, the common consensus is that he acquitted himself well. He also looked strikingly young – this was going to stand him in good stead over the coming years, not least because he was a man in his twenties who could get away with pretending to be a teenager. Even in his thirties, Eddie looks far younger than he really is.

Eddie's university band Blue Tonic might have gone nowhere fast, but it certainly helped him, as someone at the model agents Storm saw a picture of him and recognised his potential in a flash. Eddie's appearance is very well suited to modelling: not only is he tall and slim, but he has high cheekbones and full lips – features that marked him out from the crowd. Male models don't earn as much as female ones, but they certainly don't do badly either, and this was a good way to earn money while waiting for his acting career to take off (not that it would take very long). Like so many actors who start off as models – Jamie Dornan is another – Eddie remained somewhat ambivalent about his modelling career, telling one early interviewer, 'It was only really one big campaign, for Burberry in Europe. And I got to meet David Bailey, who shot me for *Arena*.' In actual fact it was going to turn out to be a little bit more than that.

Even though he might have been fresh on the scene, Eddie had stolen a march on his competitors because, courtesy of that appearance in *Twelfth Night*, he had experience. More importantly, the great Mark Rylance had taken an interest in the lad and spoken well of him. And so in no time at all, Eddie had landed the part of Jonathan Pryce's seventeen-year-old son Billy in Edward Albee's *The Goat, or Who Is Sylvia?* which started at the Almeida and transferred to the Apollo (apt name, given the play's reference to Greek tragedy) in the West End. Pryce's real-life partner Kate Fahy played the role of his wife.

The Goat, which had originally premiered two years previously in the United States, is a very dark play about an architect, Martin, who has been in a happy and monogamous marriage with his wife Stevie, until he falls in love with a goat called Sylvia. This 'affair' is exposed by a television presenter and friend of the family, Ross, who is preparing to interview Martin because of his great success as an architect, and triggers a massive display of violence from Stevie, who in a highly symbolic manner destroys the family's sitting room. Meanwhile the son, Billy, also becomes aware of what has happened, professing deep and terrible shock and finally kissing his father to display his love – a kiss that also suggests a very unhealthy relationship between father and son. The play ends when Stevie kills poor old Sylvia, thus shattering everything. As a first step into an acting career, Eddie could hardly have chosen a more draining role.

The play alludes to the concept of Greek tragedy (in Greek, 'tragedy' originally meant 'goat-song') and contains references to *Eumenides*, Aeschylus's play of the same name, and the Greek deities of vengeance; it took what was an apparently normal suburban setting and subverted it into something terrible and dark. Also in the manner of Greek tragedy, it took a man at the height of his powers and destroyed him. The play made a huge sensation on both sides of the Atlantic, among other things disproving the fashionable notion that tragedies weren't being written any more.

The critics absolutely loved both the production and Eddie, whose Etonian training in being able to lose any self-consciousness and access something dark within himself served him very well indeed. 'Albee's own reckoning with the Eumenides referred to in passing distributes no small amount of pain to Kate Fahy, Pryce's real-life partner, in the essentially reactive role of the wife, Stevie,' wrote *Variety*. 'Also to a blazing young actor, Eddie Redmayne, who plays the couple's seventeen-year-old gay son, Billy, with such harrowing conviction that the play now seems just as much the kid's (sorry) tragedy as mom and dad's.'

Other critics agreed. Writing in *The Guardian*, Michael Billington was a little hesitant about the husband and wife but very positive about the other two: 'Matthew Marsh as the bluntly disbelieving best friend and Eddie Redmayne as Martin's gay, emotionally fraught son are more in tune with Albee's rhythms,' he wrote. 'And by the end one is emotionally drained.'

'Eddie Redmayne as confused son Billy is plainly a star in the making,' wrote a perceptive Brian Clover in *CurtainUp. com*.

Amanda Hodges, in *LondonTheatre.co.uk*, was even more lavish in her praise. 'Eddie Redmayne, who anchors the play, gives a sensitive and pitch perfect performance as the teenage son torn between love for his parents and revulsion at the event that has driven them apart,' she wrote.

Others reached for the superlatives. *The Independent*'s Paul Taylor wrote that Eddie was 'the most electrically alive person on stage' and the *Standard*'s Nicholas de Jongh said 'he outclasses everyone with the convincing extremity of his rage, sexual confusion and vehement guilt.' The message was clear: a major new talent had arrived on the London stage.

But it also presented Eddie with his first taste of what it can be like when a production ends and there isn't a new one lined up (*Twelfth Night* didn't count, as Eddie was still at Cambridge). Acting is an insecure profession, after all, and despite being feted in that role, there was no certainty that another would come along. 'The day after *The Goat* finished I saw them stripping the posters off the walls,' he told *The Independent on Sunday*. 'After a few drinks I went running round the back streets of Soho to see if I could find a left-over poster to remind myself it hadn't all been a wonderful dream.' In the event, he didn't actually have to wait that long for a new role. He was on an upward trajectory and making waves in everything he did.

He was keeping an eye open for television opportunities, too, and another of these came when he appeared as Southampton in one episode of the two-part 2005 television mini-series *Elizabeth I*, written by Nigel Williams. He was in very good company indeed: Helen Mirren played the Virgin Queen and other actors involved included Hugh Dancy, Toby Jones, Ian McDiarmid and Jeremy Irons. The story depicted the last twenty-four years of her forty-five-year reign, with the first episode centred on her relationship with the Earl of Leicester (Irons) and the second on her relationship with the Earl of Essex (Dancy), which ends when he tries to lead a failed rebellion against her and is beheaded. The series garnered interest from both sides of the Atlantic and got, on the whole, a very positive reception. Alessandra Stanley of *The New York Times* said that Mirren was 'one of the few actresses working today who can actually convincingly play a historical figure in her forties [though its] interpretation, like so many others, wallows in the painful self-pity of a powerful, aging woman who craves true love. [It is] no match for the 1998 movie [but offers] a richly drawn portrait of a powerful woman who is both ruthless and sentimental, formidable and mercurial, vain and likable.'

David Wiegand of the *San Francisco Chronicle* was a fan. He described Mirren's portrayal as 'powerful enough to shatter your television screen, not to mention any notion you might have had that if you've seen one Elizabeth – Bette Davis, Glenda Jackson or Cate Blanchett, for example – you've seen them all ... Irons has sometimes settled into craggy self-parody in lesser films [...] invests Leicester with as much depth and complexity as he can, and he is every bit Mirren's equal onscreen.'

Brian Lowry of *Variety* said that '[director] Tom Hooper, who previously directed Mirren in *Prime Suspect 6*, indulges Williams' penchant for long, theatrical monologues, which require a little getting used to in the slow early going. Gradually, however, as with the best British costume drama, the narrative becomes absorbing.' A triumph then, for the entire cast.

Eddie learned a lot from it and not just about acting. He told an anecdote about it with his customary good humour and it turned out there was one thing he hadn't been taught at Eton. 'Last thing in the audition, as I was walking out,' he told *Esquire* magazine, 'the director, Tom Hooper, said, "Eddie, have you ever been on a horse?" I said, "Yes." Cut to Lithuania, two weeks later, a huge Elizabethan street, Helen Mirren at the end of it on a balcony, in a huge Elizabethan dress, Tom, cameras, Jeremy Irons, rain machines, fifty Lithuanian extras, spurs attached to my feet, and I'm thinking, "At what point do I tell them that I have never, ever ridden a horse?" It was then that I realised a big part of the cliché of actors lying in auditions, is that you should probably try to do the thing you said you can do before filming starts. Anyway, I nearly killed people as the horse galloped off at a hundred miles an hour after I gave it the slightest nudge. Tom came out with his megaphone and shouted, "You're a fucking liar, Redmayne!"'

The theatre was also still playing a hugely important role in Eddie's life. In those early days, rather than simply concentrating on trying to get into the mega-productions in the West End, he was taking part in productions in smaller theatres, which were able to put on more experimental or independent work. Fittingly perhaps, given the echoes of Greek tragedy in the play he had just been performing in, Eddie went for the real thing, appearing as the ghost of Polydorus, son of Hecuba, in Euripides's *Hecuba* with Clare Higgins in the title role (at the Donmar Warehouse, another small theatre known for its groundbreaking work). This play – in this case a translation by Frank McGuinness – tells the story of the deaths of Hecuba's children: Polydorus, at the hands of the Thracian king Polymestor, to whom he had been sent for safekeeping, and Polyxena, who is to be sacrificed on the tomb of Achilles. That sacrifice takes up the first part of the play, while Hecuba's revenge on Polymestor occupies the second half. As with *The Goat*, it is not for the faint-hearted.

Somewhat unusually, the ghost of Polydorus opens the proceedings with a monologue about his death; the director Jonathan Kent had Eddie rising unexpectedly from the waters of the sea, catching the audience's attention from the start. Eddie was good-natured about it. 'That pool is a feat of engineering,' he told *The Independent on Sunday*. 'But the other day I followed the pipe attached to it all the way backstage ... It only lead to the bog! So I rather pointedly asked the stage manager, um, you're not actually filling the pool with bog water are you?'

The production came just a couple of years after the invasion of Iraq and had clearly influenced director Jonathan Kent's interpretation. 'Though far from the best known or most popular of Euripides's ninety-odd plays, I knew we would get to *Hecuba* in the end, and sure enough it opened last night at the Donmar on a breathtaking seashore of a set complete with dramatic waves and tides,' wrote Sheridan Morley in the *Sunday Express*. 'The war in Iraq, or at any rate its aftermath, has made Greeks of us all ... the feeling generally still seems to be that 2,000 years ago the Greeks did it better – so back we go across the centuries, in this case to a blood-soaked saga of the Queen of Troy and her lust for revenge when it becomes clear that the invading Greeks have not only sacked her city but also put most of her family to the sword.'

More praise came from Paul Taylor in *The Independent*.

'On Paul Brown's austerely beautiful set, a raked beach leads down to a pool, representing the sea from which a soused Eddie Redmayne alarmingly emerges at the start as the ghost of Polydorus,' he wrote. 'He's the son Hecuba had hoped to save by secreting him in Thrace, but he too has been murdered (from greed for gold) by his supposed protector King Polymestor (a nicely sly Finbar Lynch).

'The production is rich in moments that make you shudder. One of the most powerful is when the one-woman Chorus (Susan Engel) finds the young man's washed-up corpse. Not realising yet what has been discovered, Clare Higgins's magnificent Hecuba pooh-poohs the Chorus's lamentation. "That is an old song. I've heard it before," she cries with blasé contempt – whereupon the Chorus creepily confides the irony of the situation into the corpse's ear.'

Kate Bassett in *The Independent On Sunday* was another fan. 'In a far more tragic realm, a boy in white rises out of the limpid sea, breaking the hush at the start of Euripides' *Hecuba*,' she wrote. 'This youth, beautifully played by Eddie Redmayne in Jonathan Kent's production, is delicate and dignified. Yet his words are fevered as he repeats that he is Priam's son, Polydorus, and is dead. In fact, there is no clean beginning for anyone in this revenge tragedy played out in the wake of the Trojan War, for Polydorus has been murdered by his guardian, Polymestor, and his royal mother, Clare Higgins's Hecuba, is a prisoner of the Greeks … Paul Brown's set design is elementally simple yet startling. A white dune slopes down to the water. Behind is a jagged wall which, when underlit, is a memorial chalked with hundreds of names – not just Trojan and Greek but Muslim, Jewish, Hispanic etc.'

The role in *Hecuba* was to prove the stepping stone to Eddie's first film, *Like Minds* (also known as *Murderous Intent*). Eddie had the starring role of Alex Forbes and the film was shot in Yorkshire and South Australia, giving Eddie his first taste of something else, too: the amount of travelling a successful actor has to do, especially if they are working on a film. The plot, which plays out in flashback, centred round Alex's time at a boarding school where his father is headmaster and also a member of a secret society; into this mix steps fellow student Nigel, who has an obsession with dead things and whose father is in the same secret society as Alex's. Nigel very soon ends up dead and a psychologist played by Toni Collette is called in to see if Alex should stand trial for murder; he seems strangely indifferent to it all, and it is only revealed slowly that Nigel had been convinced that the two of them were descendants of the Knights Templar and had to commit a ritualistic murder of a schoolgirl, played by Kate Maberly, to gain enormous powers. As the story plays out, it further emerges that Alex's father also has some rather disturbing secrets.

Eddie was characteristically enthusiastic but given that this was his first film, it would have been strange if he hadn't been. 'We were filming in Sydney. It's about two psychotic seveteen-year-olds, played by Tom [Sturridge] and me, and their symbiotic relationship,' he told one interviewer. 'It was a very exciting project and my first feature film. The only downside was that my girlfriend [Tara] was back in London … She marches me down to the shops to buy newspapers when I've got reviews coming out.'

Although it was a low-budget film and didn't attract much attention, the response was positive as far as Eddie's performance was concerned, with Richard Kuipers in *Variety* writing, 'Armed with more imagination than most thrillers with teen protags, Oz-U.K. co-prod *Like Minds* is an intriguing whodunit centered on two privileged British schoolboys with an unhealthy interest in the Knights Templar … Redmayne steps up to the plate with a chilling perf as the boy with psychopathic tendencies.'

Alan Frank in the *Daily Star* also liked it. 'This is one of those rare movies that grabs you right from the start and keeps you wanting to know what's going to happen next. Redmayne is a truly nerve-jangling character and Tom Sturridge scores as his victim … The ever-twisting story, which kicks off intriguingly as Redmayne coolly confesses to Collette: "He had to die – it was a necessary means to an end", is consistently complex, compelling and generates stark suspense that scrapes your nerves.'

Many critics thought that Eddie was the best thing in the film. James Mottram, of Film4, perceptively opined, 'The type of film that will be looked back on as a notable starting point for its young star, *Like Minds* is a perfect showcase for his talent, but less so for writer-director Read, who allows the script to career out of control in the second half.'

Peter Bradshaw in *The Guardian* felt much the same: 'Eddie Redmayne is very good as the prime suspect: icily detached, taunting the investigating officers, playing them along, as if Hannibal Lecter had turned up in a production of *Another Country*,' he wrote. 'It's good stuff from Redmayne, but the plot unravels into muddle and absurdity.' Anna Smith, in *Time Out*, got straight to the point: 'Toni Collette must have owed the director quite a favour,' she wrote.

According to Edward Porter in *The Sunday Times*, it had aimed high but hadn't quite got there. 'Although the dreaded Knights Templar get a mention, the film is more concerned with psychopathy than with supernatural scares,' he wrote. 'The writer/director, Gregory Read, was clearly aiming for something more sophisticated than the average teen horror, but the result is dull and has no hope of reaching beyond a young audience.'

Wendy Ide in *The Times* hated it, writing, 'It's utterly unconvincing and sunk by several shockingly bad performances – the Australian Richard Roxburgh is particularly dreadful as a shouty British police detective. The real problem however is the brain-numbingly lethargic pacing and the interminable running time.' You can't please everybody – a lesson that Eddie, as an actor, was certainly destined to learn.

However, he learned from the experience and was full of praise for his fellow actors. 'My first film, *Like Minds*, was with Toni Collette, who was extraordinary,' he told *The Independent*. 'I mean it was basically a mini-masterclass for acting on film at a time when all you could probably see were my eyebrows bouncing up and down on screen.'

It must be said, however, that in an interview that Eddie did in 2008, he also commented, 'When I started off doing film, I did some bad work that I wasn't happy with.' No names were mentioned, but it wasn't too hard to guess what he was talking about.

Whatever the critics might have thought, Eddie was beginning to attract notice from a wider audience. He appeared in a 'Stars of Tomorrow' feature in *The Times*, with the paper commenting on his mix of delicate beauty and proven acting talent. He also got a mention in the *Daily Star* about Hollywood stars of tomorrow. The romance with Tara was continuing, confounding some people who thought, presumably because of his slightly feminine features, that he was gay, and the two of them turned up to first nights and events together, as Eddie became increasingly well-known.

And indeed, his career continued to go swimmingly. His theatre work had attracted the attention of quite a number of casting agents and one in particular put him forward for another film, one that was in a different league from *Like Minds*. Written by Eric Roth, *The Good Shepherd* was a film that Robert De Niro, no less, was looking to direct, co-produce and also play a small role in. De Niro was alerted to this major new talent on the London stage and Eddie was summoned into his presence, something that both delighted and terrified him at the same time.

'She [the casting director] said, "I want you to come back

and meet Bob this afternoon." I was like, Who? "Bob De Niro." F**k,' he told *M* magazine.

'When I came back, the casting couch was full of the best actors in Britain, all in their fifties and sixties; people who never audition for anything were lined. I was the only kid there. I went in and met De Niro.'

De Niro wanted him to part his hair: 'Iwanyataparyerhair,' was how Eddie relayed it. And then, as if he were not already terrified enough, Leonardo di Caprio (who was not in the film but who had originally been slated for the main role) turned up and read the role of his father for the audition. 'I was absolutely wetting myself. I looked down at the scene, from the ceiling, and said to myself, "Redmayne, if you die now, you've had it pretty good." From there, I just turned up and tried not to get fired.'

Filming began and this pitched Eddie into a totally new league: that of big-shot Hollywood players and a lifestyle very far removed from experimental theatre in London. 'Suddenly I'm flying across the Atlantic and staying at hotels in New York and being taken to work in SUVs with blacked out windows,' he told *Hollywood.com*. 'I arrived at the studio and there's Angelina Jolie and Matt Damon and there's tons of paparazzi outside. Everywhere I looked there was a famous person and suddenly there's a camera in my face and Robert De Niro behind it, going, "And act!" I was so frightened basically of getting fired that when you watch the film I just look terrified! The character was meant to look terrified but not that terrified! I auditioned for many months and in the end I basically got the job because I have big lips and I was playing Angelina Jolie's son!'

He was being too modest: Eddie was fast becoming one of the most talked-about actors in town, but in this particular film Angelina Jolie and Matt Damon were the stars. A piece of fiction based on real events, the film was billed as being about the untold story of the beginning of the CIA, with the Edward Wilson character (Matt Damon) based on James Jesus Angleton and Richard M. Bissell. Posing the question 'Who is the good shepherd? The one who looks after his family or the one who looks after his country?', the film centres on Wilson. He was the head of CIA operations during the Bay of Pigs, the failed military invasion of Cuba by the CIA-sponsored Brigade 2506 in 1961, which heralded the Cuban Missile Crisis. Wilson becomes convinced that a double agent within the CIA tipped Cuba's President Castro off and as he searches for the offender, he recalls incidents in his life via a series of flashbacks. These include his father's death, his time as a student and recruitment into the service, his love affairs and marriage, his distant relationship with his son (Eddie) and the growing Cold War. Along the way, his character changes and develops, as his idealism inevitably alters in the light of all he experiences, and paranoia begins to take hold.

Although some liked it, it wasn't really a great success. Kenneth Turan remarked in the *Los Angeles Times*, 'Damon, in his second major role of the year (after *The Departed*) once again demonstrates his ability to convey emotional reserves, to animate a character from the inside out and create a man we can sense has more of an interior life than he is willing to let on.' But Manohla Dargis said in *The New York Times* that, '*The Good Shepherd* is an origin story about the C.I.A., and for the filmmakers that story boils down to fathers who fail their sons, a suspect metaphor that here becomes all too ploddingly literal [but] Among the film's most striking visual tropes is the image of Wilson simply going to work in the capital alongside other similarly dressed men, a spectral army clutching briefcases and silently marching to uncertain victory.'

Peter Travers of *Rolling Stone* magazine was harsher: 'It's tough to slog through a movie that has no pulse.' Similarly, Joe Emerson wrote in the *Chicago Sun-Times*, 'If you think George Tenet's Central Intelligence Agency was a disaster, wait until you see Robert De Niro's torpid, ineffectual movie about the history of the agency.' Peter Bradshaw in *The Guardian* was likewise displeased: 'And why is Damon allowed to act in such a callow, boring way? As ever, he looks like he is playing Robin to some imaginary Batman at his side, like Jimmy Stewart and his invisible rabbit. His nasal, unobtrusive voice makes every line sound the same.'

But there were some positives. In *The New York Observer*, Andrew Sarris was kinder: 'Still, no previous American film has ventured into this still largely unknown territory with such authority and emotional detachment. For this reason alone, *The Good Shepherd* is must-see viewing.' *USA Today* was also won over: 'What makes the story work so powerfully is his focus on a multidimensional individual

– Wilson – thereby creating a stirring personal tale about the inner workings of the clandestine government agency.' And *Time* magazine's Richard Corliss was similarly well disposed: 'Damon is terrific in the role-all-knowing, never overtly expressing a feeling. Indeed, so is everyone else in this intricate, understated but ultimately devastating account of how secrets, when they are left to fester, can become an illness, dangerous to those who keep them, more so to nations that base their policies on them.'

David Ansen of *Newsweek* felt that it started quite brilliantly and then went off: 'For the film's mesmerizing first fifty minutes I thought De Niro might pull off the Godfather of spy movies … Still, even if the movie's vast reach exceeds its grasp, it's a spellbinding history lesson.'

But the lacklustre reviews didn't matter for Eddie: he was on a roll. His part as Billy in *The Goat* handed him the Outstanding Newcomer Award at the 50th Evening Standard Theatre Awards, and indeed things were going so well for him that he began to dread that it would all fall apart. 'This has been an amazingly lucky year for me, with the award as its climax,' he told during one interview, 'and I know that it has come too easily. Friends who went to drama school are aware of how competitive the business can be, but because I have been cotton-wooled into it I'm literally living the dream at the moment. That will implode at some point, and whether I can deal with that, I don't know.' He didn't have to worry, though. It was not a situation he was going to have to face anytime soon.

CHAPTER FIVE

TAKING RISKS

The Good Shepherd might not have been Eddie's finest hour (or anyone else's, come to that) but it had given him a taste for cinema and so he decided to embark on a career that was to combine mainstream films (some mainstream films, at least – there were also a lot of arthouse choices) with quirkier theatrical outings, as very many actors before him have done. The great Laurence Olivier used to say that he took part in Hollywood productions in order to fund his theatre work in the UK, and Eddie split himself in a similar fashion, although in fairness, much of Eddie's later film work would be as serious and as good as anything he did on the stage.

For someone who was to make such an impact in his later films, his earlier choices were interesting, to put it politely.

But to his great credit, Eddie was showing that he would not shy away from controversial material: he was prepared to tackle themes that other actors would have avoided. And that early training at Eton, allowing him to be fearless in his acting, was now beginning to propel him forward, even if his choices were not always the best. Eddie had to serve his time as a jobbing actor to a certain extent and it was only as he reached his late twenties that his name began to ring bells with the wider public, but his rise through the profession was actually pretty fast.

Another film he made around the same time, *Savage Grace*, with Julianne Moore, was arguably a far better film. It was based on the true story of Barbara Daly Baekeland: a very unstable socialite married to Brooks Baekeland (played by Stephen Dillane) who was eventually murdered by her schizophrenic son Antony, played by Eddie, in London in 1972. It was a shocking cause célèbre at the time it happened and made headlines all over the world. It was clear that the mother was almost as unstable as her son; indeed, the whole family had been troubled: her father had committed suicide, her mother had had a mental breakdown before her birth, and Barbara was a demanding and emotional woman, given to scenes and recrimination. It had also been known for years that Antony had severe mental problems but his father, who didn't believe in psychiatry, didn't allow him to be treated.

The marriage between the young couple was characterised by numerous affairs on both sides and a peripatetic lifestyle that had the couple moving all over the world – an unstable existence that seemed to depend on a desperate desire to be the centre of attention wherever they happened to pitch up. It would not have been the ideal way to bring up a child under the best of circumstances, but matters were made far, far worse by the totally inexplicable behaviour of the mother who was, however, almost certainly mentally ill.

The most shocking aspect was this: Barbara was alleged to have had an incestuous affair with her son, possibly, according to some observers, as a way of trying to 'cure' him of his homosexuality. Another theory is that as Antony himself became increasingly violent and troubled – although his mother was certain he could never hurt her – this was a bizarre way on her part to try to calm him down.

The film did not shy away from any of this; its trajectory charted Antony's life, from his birth to the murder, and it was nothing if not a brave choice for Eddie, for it was hardly a role to which most people could relate, given that it encompassed not one, but two taboos: incest and matricide. It was also a brave choice for Julianne Moore. Although the film ended with the killing, in real life Antony was charged with murder and spent eight years in Broadmoor psychiatric hospital before being released and returning to New York, where he attempted to kill his maternal grandmother, Nina Daly. He was again arrested and committed suicide in his cell.

All in all, it was a highly controversial subject matter and everyone involved was quite upfront about it. Even director Tom Kalin recognised that this would not be to everyone's taste. 'That oedipal bond between the two of them is what made the film attractive in the first place,' he told *The Daily Telegraph*. 'It was sensational, shocking, true-life material, but it also had the resonance of Greek tragedy.' As for the lengthy sex scene between mother and son, he commented, 'I've had some quite intense reactions. "Why the hell are you putting it on screen for this long?" Because I think it's necessary dramatically, to get to that place where you see what's going on between the characters. The detachment of intimacy. He's all strung out, chain smoking, when she comes home. It's sort of lion taming. She calms him down by having sex with him.' That reference to Greek tragedy mirrored *The Goat* – it could be said that Eddie's classical education was very much drawing him to these roles.

Julianne Moore, whose part was just as difficult and controversial as Eddie's, spoke about what drew her to the project and also saw within it elements of the type of tragedy that stretches back for thousands of years. And it was quite a role for a mainstream Hollywood A-lister to take on. 'I was very interested in this story,' she told *The Mirror*. 'It's a really classic tragedy of a family destroying itself. Barbara has a history of depression and several suicide attempts. Her father committed suicide, her brother committed suicide and she was probably manic-depressive. Tony was a diagnosed schizophrenic, so clearly there was a tremendous amount of mental illness in the family, as well as drug use and excessive wealth – you name it! Obviously you do have some trepidation about that kind of stuff [the incest scene]. But it's not being celebrated. This is presented as a tragedy.'

Eddie had badly wanted the role, while conceding that not everyone was going to enjoy watching it. He appeared to be actively pursuing difficult subject matter, aware, perhaps, that it was a good way to establish a reputation as a serious actor and that it was also going to get him noticed faster than a more anodyne role would. 'That was a really special project for me, which I chased and chased and chased, and finally got, thanks to Tom Kalin, the director, and to Julianne,' he told *Interview* magazine. 'It's one of those scripts that you read and you become sort of embarrassingly protective of it, like, "Please don't let anyone else get this!" ... it's also the kind I love. In England we have this saying about Marmite: people either love it or hate it. That's like a lot of the movie work I've done. People either find it repulsive or find it really interesting and get engaged in it.' The fact that he was prepared to do work that some people would not be able to stomach also stood him in good stead.

But this type of work would have been difficult for any actor, especially one who was still really starting out in his career. On another occasion some years later, he explained how he had prepared for the film's pivotal scene – a sex scene with, of course, the added twist that it was between him and his on-screen mother. How could anyone get ready for that? 'It really depends on the actor,' he said and it turned out that his co-star had taken a slightly different approach. 'Some will spend the whole day locked up and some will use humour. I remember doing this movie *Savage Grace*. There's this really intense love scene with Julianne Moore who plays my mum. For weeks, I had been reading these disturbing things and my character is kind of freaking out at some point. But Julianne was in such a normal chatty mood and I had to be brooding. On that specific day, the character is going mad, I had to keep going to a corner of the room whereas she was absolutely laughing all the time. I felt a bit of a dick for doing that but there are other days where it's the other way round.'

Eddie was often to speak in later years about how much he'd benefitted from working with older and more experienced actors, and being able to watch the way they worked close-up, as had been the case in this film. 'Stephen is incredibly cerebral and has a meticulous way of rehearsing,' he told *The Independent*. 'Julianne is a shooter from the hip – she doesn't like to go straight into scene. And as the kid, I was sitting there thinking, "Oh my God these are two hugely different ways of working." But that was wonderful for capturing the character of a boy who is pulled in two directions ...'

And what did his own mother think about it? The Redmaynes, while extremely supportive of their talented boy, were not a theatrical family and although they clearly knew that it was acting, they had to face some rather disquieting scenes, which were not made any easier by the fact that a family member was involved. However, this was not, it emerged, the first time his family had had to put up with potentially awkward scenes, since he had also performed them on stage. 'Ahha,' said Eddie, who must have been asked about this a fair few times. 'You know what's really funny is for my first play *The Goat*, in London, I was playing a young gay New Yorker. In the last scene, I had to kiss Jonathan Pryce who played my dad. My brothers would come and watch the play in order to watch my dad's reaction. It was a funny thing. And when there was a film festival for *Savage Grace*, my family were there to watch my mum ... I feel I put my parents through a lot. Bless them; because they don't come from this world, I think they are so shocked that I actually get work. They are very supportive. They're like "if this is what you need to get work, go ahead".' They were in fact increasingly proud that Eddie was succeeding in such a difficult and competitive field.

The film duly came out and the critical reception was mixed, not least because of that difficult subject matter, but at any rate most people seemed to respect the integrity of the crew, who had tried to tell such a dark tale. And some were lavish in their praise. Peter Bradshaw in *The Guardian* was one critic who was extremely impressed. 'A sick-room torpor hangs heavily about this masterfully controlled, elegantly composed movie by Tom Kalin, his first full-length feature since the much-admired *Swoon* from 1992,' he wrote. 'It is a sensational, lurid story: erotic and repulsive by overlapping turn. And it's pulp fact.' The fact that it was based on a true story was indeed fascinating to many – had the plot been invented, it might well have been deemed just too over the top to be true.

Bradshaw was not alone – Bruce Demara in the *Toronto*

Star was similarly impressed. 'While the pace occasionally flags and there are times when we wonder where Kalin is leading us, he maintains a pervasive sense of dread and unease throughout that makes the chilling climax seem both shocking and inevitable.' And Liam Lacey of *The Globe and Mail* felt that, 'Though the characters may be repellent, the film permits you to feel sympathy.'

But they were in the minority, as others were unmoved. 'A film as harsh, brittle and unbalanced as its characters,' said *Empire* magazine. 'It's a horror story, all right, but the reason for telling it remains unclear, and it seems like a waste of Kalin's evident talent,' wrote Walter V. Addiego in the *San Francisco Chronicle*. And Dennis Schwartz of *Ozus' World Movie Reviews* dismissed it as a 'superficial dysfunctional story on the rich'. But as ever, Eddie was gaining experience and learning his trade. In later years he seemed to take pride in it, not least because the subject matter was so dark and yet everyone involved had still been determined to tell the tale.

In the light of Eddie's later success, it is easy to forget that not everything ran as smoothly as he wanted it to. His reputation was growing but, like so many actors before him, he had to supplement his income with more menial jobs – and he did that in the time-honoured fashion, too. Asked by *The Independent* what had been his worst ever job, he replied, 'I worked as a waiter at the British Soap Awards for the BBC. They feed all these soap stars with alcohol and then put them in the studio for the awards so they're more rowdy and it makes for better television.

'So, as a waiter, I had to stand there with a tray waiting for them to put their empties on before going in. I remember this whole group of actors from *Hollyoaks* piling on with loads of Champagne glasses and it being full, and one of them saying "Guys, guys, watch this! I'm going to put one more on, I'm going to put one more on ..." And I was thinking, "No, please don't put another ..." and them smashing everywhere. All these *Hollyoaks* actors were in hysterics and I was like, "You bastards!"'

But these memories were becoming a thing of the past. Alongside his film career, there was also the growing theatrical one; once more, Eddie was happy to take on controversial roles – and again, ended up playing someone's son in difficult circumstances. He looked a little younger than his years at that point and so roles revolving around sons were a pretty obvious choice. In this case the play was called *Now or Later* and it was put on at the Royal Court. Written by the New York playwright Christopher Shinn and directed by Dominic Cooke, it was about the US elections: Eddie played the gay twenty-year-old son of a candidate who, disturbed by what is going on around him, somewhat controversially attends a party dressed as the prophet Muhammad. Photos go on to surface, which doesn't bode well for either father or son. The people running his father's campaign want him to apologise and the play is essentially an argument of ideas: should John apologise for what was his own political act?

'He is the son of the Democratic nominee for the election in 2008, and his dad is about to be elected president,' Eddie told *The Guardian*. 'And it's election night, and my character has gone and done something which is perceived by most people as being incredibly foolish. And it's about to turn pretty hardcore and basically have massive international ramifications.'

Eddie went on to confide that the role took him back to his own student days. 'What I do remember is this idea of sparring with friends, arguments about issues and current affairs,' he said. 'I'm a pretty poor arguer, but there are those moments when you suddenly realise that you've taken a standpoint, and you've so been pushed into a corner, and you're actually beginning to believe what you're saying more than you ever actually meant. And that is something I kept finding in this play. There are moments where I really did think [John Jr] was going to apologise, but the more people press him, the more he feels cornered. He's like a hedgehog.'

Eddie met Cherie Blair in the course of preparing for the role, in order to ask her about the tricky subject of combining politics with family life. 'She was fascinating about the importance of family, and about trying to keep a family away from the spotlight,' he said. 'It's the idea that kids make mistakes, and if you're a parent they're just something that a sixteen or seventeen-year-old would do. But of course, if you're in power those ramifications are going to be much greater. It's kind of the parent's issue, for having become a public figure.' Did her own children voice opinions? 'She came up with what was a really valid comment: "I believe absolutely that you have the right to hear people's opinions, but also that you have to have more belief in people who will actually go out and do something about that opinion. You must also be proactive with it." Kids that are born into families where their lives have a predestined quality is one thing, like royalty or massive landowners. But when your parents have chosen to go into that world, it's another deal.'

Critical response was mixed. *The Independent*'s Paul Taylor loved it; calling it unmissable, he wrote that 'Eddie Redmayne is superb. Eyes glittering with wit and wounded sensitivity, he shows how John is both damaged goods and the goods. There's a wonderful moment when, after a phone call from his former therapist, he reveals that he thought it was going to be from the boyfriend who recently dumped him. His face fights a great dam-burst of tears and you ache for him.'

Philip Fisher of *British Theatre Guide* was also impressed. 'Eddie Redmayne gives a finely judged and very sensitive performance as preppy John, the son of the Democrat who has just been elected President of the United States of America,' he wrote. 'The action takes place in his bare, unimpressive hotel room on election night as state after state declares support for his father, another (much more grizzled) John, played by Matthew Marsh ... This all works well as drama and gives Shinn a platform to debate the knotty question of the extent to which Americans should now work with or pander to Islam but also challenges the failure to embrace homosexuality even among ostensible liberals.'

The Guardian's film critic, Michael Billington, while kind enough about it all, had reservations. 'There is enough matter here for a good ding-dong debate, which Shinn duly delivers,' he wrote. 'But, in making a John a gay man with a past history of nervous disorder and serious quarrels with his father's vote-seeking shift to the right, Shinn introduces enough issues to fuel a three-act play. The play undeniably keeps you rapt. And, although Eddie Redmayne as the defiant John has a habit of dropping his voice at the end of sentences, he conveys all the character's gangling, principled obduracy ... I simply found that absorbing so many complex arguments in such a short span made my head spin.'

The play had all the hallmarks of the work Eddie was interested in at the time, of course: the troubled father-son relationship, incipient tragedy, controversial subject matter and an intelligent debate about difficult issues. But he was beginning to take on much more mainstream work, as well.

As with so many other actors of his generation, Eddie was not just confining himself to stage and screen: he was taking part in television productions as well. Some of the finest drama, both in the United Kingdom and the United States was taking place on the small screen; an example of this was *Homeland*, whose first three seasons starred Damian Lewis and which was – at least for the first season and possibly the second – widely considered to be a stunning success. Actors did also feel that they did not have to limit themselves to just one medium anymore. Whereas previously they worked either on television or film, the first sometimes leading to the second, it had until quite recently been the case that they didn't usually work for both. That had changed, though, and by the time Eddie came on the scene, some very famous actors were regularly appearing on both.

But back in the film world, Eddie was to revisit ground he had trodden very recently, namely the Elizabethan era. Cate Blanchett had been persuaded to make a sequel to her very successful 1998 film *Elizabeth*; this new film, which played fast and loose with historical reality was called *Elizabeth: the Golden Age* and covered the latter part of Elizabeth's reign. To cut a long story short, yet again Elizabeth is forced to accept her role as the Virgin Queen and reject the bonds of holy matrimony after her favourite, Sir Walter Raleigh, runs off with someone else. Meanwhile, Mary Queen of Scots is plotting trouble in the background.

Eddie played Anthony Babington, one of the traitors who conspired with Mary to bring Elizabeth down. He formulated the Babington Plot, which ultimately led to Mary's execution and indeed his own, via a particularly grisly method, after which parts of the co-conspirators bodies were hung all over London to show exactly what kind of fate lay in store for a traitor to the queen.

When the film came out, it was actually subject to charges of being anti-Catholic, mainly due to the fact that it was representing a period when Catholics (Queen Mary) and Protestants (Queen Elizabeth) really were at war. But there was some real anger out there. 'The climax, a weakly staged destruction of the Spanish Armada, is a crescendo of church-bashing imagery: rosaries floating amid burning flotsam, inverted crucifixes sinking to the bottom of the ocean, the rows of ominous be-robed clerics slinking away in defeat,' wrote Steven D. Greydanus in the *National Catholic Register*. 'Pound for pound, minute for minute, *Elizabeth: The Golden Age* could possibly contain more sustained church-bashing than any other film I can think of. How is it possible that this orgy of anti-Catholicism has been all but ignored by most critics?'

Some very senior and important figures agreed. Franco Cardini, who was a historian at the University of Florence, said that 'the film formed part of a "concerted attack on Catholicism, the Holy See and Papism" ... Why put out this perverse anti-Catholic propaganda today, just at the moment when we are trying desperately to revive our Western identity in the face of the Islamic threat, presumed or real?'

Unsurprisingly, director Shekhar Kapur totally rejected any accusations of anti-Catholicism, stating that the opposite was true. 'It is actually very, very deeply non-anti-Catholic,' he said. 'It is anti extreme forms of religion. At that time the Church in Spain, or Philip, had said that they were going to turn the whole world into a very pure form of Catholicism. So it's not anti-Catholic. It's anti an interpretation of the word of God that is singular, as against what Elizabeth's was, which was to look upon her faith as concomitant. The fact is that the Pope ordered her execution; he said that anybody who executes or assassinates Elizabeth would find a beautiful place in the kingdom of heaven. Where else have you heard these words about Salman Khan or Salman

Rushdie? That's why I made this film, so this idea of a rift between Catholicism and Protestants does not arise.'

Anti-Catholic or no, while Cate's performance was praised – and she was nominated for an Oscar – the film was not the critical success that its predecessor had been. One person who loved it, however, was Michael Gove (who went on to become a very prominent Conservative politician) on the grounds that it was a far more positive and patriotic take on British history than that which is so often seen today. 'It tells the story of England's past in a way which someone who's familiar with the Whig tradition of history would find, as I did, completely sympathetic,' he said on BBC2's *Newsnight Review*. 'It's amazing to see a film made now that is so patriotic ... One of the striking things about this film is that it's almost a historical anomaly. I can't think of a historical period film in which England and the English have been depicted heroically for the last forty or fifty years. You almost have to go back to Laurence Olivier's Shakespeare's *Henry V* in which you actually have an English king and English armies portrayed heroically.'

But while he was not alone in his views, he certainly wasn't in the majority. Peter Bradshaw of *The Guardian* was scathing: 'Where Kapur's first Elizabeth was cool, cerebral, fascinatingly concerned with complex plotting, the new movie is pitched at the level of a Jean Plaidy romantic novel.' Roger Ebert was no keener: 'There are scenes where the costumes are so sumptuous, the sets so vast, the music so insistent, that we lose sight of the humans behind the dazzle of the production. [But] That Blanchett could appear in the same Toronto Film Festival playing Elizabeth and Bob Dylan [a reference to the film *I'm Not There*], both splendidly, is a wonder of acting.'

Colin Covert of the *Star Tribune* (of Minneapolis) felt that 'as a pseudo-historical fable, a romantic triangle and a blood-and-thunder melodrama, the film can't be faulted.' He also added, 'This isn't historical fabrication, it's mutilation. But for all its lapses, this is probably the liveliest, most vibrant Elizabethan production since Baz Luhrmann's *Romeo + Juliet*.' Arguably, this was praise, of sorts.

It certainly wasn't a triumph, but yet again it saw Eddie working with the highest calibre of actors, continuing to learn his trade. And he was beginning to show the full scope of his range, too. He had a fine line in troubled young sons, there was no doubt about that, but here he was as a dashing young revolutionary – and this was just the start. Although he was still nowhere near being an established actor, let alone a household name, Eddie's was a moniker that was cropping up increasingly regularly from the mouths of casting directors and the movers and shakers who matter in the industry. More work was building up in the pipeline. Eddie Redmayne was on his way.

CHAPTER SIX

A ROAD TRIP
TO SUCCESS

It is fair to say that the films in which Eddie was becoming involved had yet to set the world on fire, but he was acquitting himself well enough, getting used to the business of being on film sets, and generally absorbing the atmosphere and enjoying it as he went along. His next film was to be *The Yellow Handkerchief*, a remake of a 1977 Japanese film of the same name which boasted some very big names – William Hurt, Kristen Stewart and Maria Bello were his co-stars. Although Kristen Stewart, back in 2008, was not quite the big name she is now, it was still an impressive round-up. Eddie got equal billing with the other three, with his name above the title as well.

The Yellow Handkerchief was another one that was off the beaten track: despite the cast list, it certainly wasn't blockbuster material. It was a road movie across post-Hurricane Katrina Louisiana, in which Brett Hanson (William), who has been released from prison after six years, decides to journey across the state to meet his ex-wife May (Maria), in a bid to come to terms with a difficult past. On his travels he meets two teenagers: Martine (Kristen), who is running away from her family, and geeky Gordy (Eddie). The three all have issues: will May take Brett back and does he want her to? What will be Martine's relationship with boys in general and her family? And, somewhat inevitably, will there be a relationship between Martine and Gordy? 'It's a road movie and I play an adopted Native American who maybe has Asperger's,' was Eddie's way of summing up his role. It was another challenging part but at least this one wasn't that of a disturbed son with parent issues. Undeniably, though, Eddie was carving out a reputation as someone who could portray characters who didn't fit into a conventional role, and Gordy was certainly that.

In the meantime, he was also able to watch the way another leading actor – in this case William Hurt, who took it very seriously – prepared for his role. William spent four days at Louisiana State Penitentiary, also known as Angola, including an overnight stay in a maximum security cell, which is something very rare for a volunteer. 'I spent [the] night in maximum security there. I think I'm the other person who electively has done that,' he told *Fresh Air*. 'I think someone else tried to but screamed and gave up at midnight. I spoke with every member on that row who's incarcerated in an eight-foot-by-four-foot cell twenty-three hours a day for the rest of their lives... those who would speak to me. Some wouldn't ... Claustrophobic isn't the word. It's much worse. I didn't think that I was uncomfortable most of the night. I was preoccupied with my companion, and the bed has about an inch-and-a-half-thick mattress on sheer steel. The toilet has no soft seat. The floor is marbleized concrete. It's horrible. It's unthinkable.' It was certainly a way of making sure he knew what the character he was portraying had to endure. William garnered a great deal of respect for his actions.

But there was a lighter side to it as well, as by this time Eddie had begun to discover one of the great benefits of a successful career in acting: the opportunity to travel all over the world. This time round it was in the US Deep South. 'Living in New Orleans was mind blowing,' he said. 'Living in that city and seeing it culturally and musically definitely made the film special. New Orleans is where they arrive at the end of this trip and there is a celebratory quality to it. A lot of the film is about chance. It's about how all these small interactions in life can fuse and accumulate into amazing things. It's about generosity of spirit, about looking beyond the surface of people because on the surface all four of these characters are massively flawed and yet they've all got kind, kind hearts and deep hearts. So it's about looking beyond the veneer.'

In the event, the film didn't make a huge splash, but the critics liked it well enough for its quirkiness and originality. '"The Yellow Handkerchief" is a love story,' wrote Michael

O'Sullivan in *The Washington Post*. 'Two, really. At its center is the sweetly fractured ticking of a broken heart on the mend ... On another, more literal level, that heart belongs to Brett Hanson (William Hurt) ... He is, however, very, very sad about something. ... Through flashbacks, we learn that the pain has something to do with a woman named May (Maria Bello) ... That's not the most interesting relationship in the film. That would be the off-kilter triangle that Brett suddenly finds himself in after accepting a lift from Gordy (Eddie Redmayne), an artistic teenage misfit with a beat-up convertible who takes beautiful photos using expired film, and Martine (Kristen Stewart), a girl who seems to be halfheartedly running away.'

'You don't need an original story for a movie,' wrote the great Roger Ebert. 'You need original characters and living dialogue. *The Yellow Handkerchief*, written by Erin Dignam, directed by Udayan Prasad, has those, and evocative performances. William Hurt occupies the silent center of the film ... Stewart is, quite simply, a wonderful actress. I must not hold the Twilight movies against her ... In recent film after film, she shows a sure hand and an intrinsic power. The story of Redmayne, who plays Gordy, is unexpected. He fits effortlessly into the role of the scrawny, uncertain fifteen-year-old Louisiana kid. Yet I learn he is twenty-seven, a Brit who went to Eton, a veteran of Shakespeare and Edward Albee. Michael Caine explained to me long ago why it's easier for British actors to do American accents than the other way around. Whatever. You can't find a crack in his performance here.' From one of the most revered critics in movie history, that was quite a write-up.

David Edelstein of *New York* magazine concurred, saying of Eddie, 'You'd never know this terrific young actor is a Brit.' He also added, '*The Yellow Handkerchief*'s three road warriors are essentially homeless, and Prayad, working with the great cinematographer Chris Menges, sets them down in a landscape of rusty garages and corroded shacks and storm-lashed boats ... But by the time the three drive over the bridge into New Orleans, the film has gone soft. Some movies are better when characters' mysterious backstories stay mysterious. But the spell of this one's first half carries you far, far downriver.'

And Keith Cohen of *Entertainment Spectrum* loved it: 'This uplifting film is an indie gem with a wonderful payoff that will bring you to tears,' he wrote. 'The acting is superlative and makes this emotionally moving experience good to the last drop.'

Eddie's schedule was getting very full, with plenty of work in the pipeline and more coming in all the time. He returned again to the Elizabethan age – or to be slightly more accurate, the period just before it – when he played the part of William Stafford in *The Other Boleyn Girl*. This film described the machinations of the Boleyn family to get Henry VIII (Eric Bana), who was having problems with his wife Catherine of Aragon because she had not provided him with a son, interested in their worldly daughter Anne (Natalie Portman). Although they were ultimately successful – indeed, she was the mother of Elizabeth I – Henry was initially interested in her married sister Mary (Scarlett Johansson). After much conniving, during which Henry marries Anne and then executes her, Mary ends up married to William Stafford. Apart from a return to the sixteenth century, it was also a reunion: Mark Rylance, who had given Eddie his first major career opportunity, was playing the part of Thomas Boleyn, the girls' father.

And although Eddie's role was a smaller one, he was still mixing with some very big stars. He was also learning diplomacy. Asked to choose between the two leading women, he replied, 'Genuinely? They are two completely different people. But both wonderful. Natalie [Portman] is incredibly, incredibly cute, bright and spunky. Scarlett is incredibly instinctive, beautifully smart and grown up. I couldn't believe she was younger than me! The dream woman would be a mixture of both but they are both extraordinary in their own ways. I loved working with both. Scarlett was my wife so it was the high point of my career.'

The film portrayed Anne as a schemer and Mary as a blushing ingénue, which led to some criticisms of historical inaccuracy. Some people were really quite irritated by it – and it's true that in these days when history is not taught as rigorously at school as it once was, there was the risk that some viewers might have taken this as the historical truth. 'In real life, by the time Mary Boleyn started her affair with Henry, she had already enjoyed a passionate liaison with his great rival, King François I of France,' Alex von Tunzelmann wrote in *The Guardian*. 'Rather ungallantly, François called her "my hackney", explaining that she was fun to ride. Chucked out of France by his irritated wife, Mary sashayed back to England and casually notched up her second kingly conquest. The film's portrayal of this Boleyn girl as a shy, blushing damsel could hardly be further from the truth.'

Still, there was a movie to be made. This was another one that didn't get praise across the board, but those critics who were able to see it as mainly an enjoyable romp were kind enough. 'This is an enjoyable movie with an entertaining angle on a hard-to-resist period of history,' wrote Mick LaSalle of the *San Francisco Chronicle*. 'Portman's performance, which shows a range and depth unlike anything she's done before, is the No. 1 element that tips *The Other Boleyn Girl* in the direction of a recommendation ... [She] won't get the credit she deserves for this, simply because the movie isn't substantial enough to warrant proper attention.' (That was a perceptive review – the film came out several years before *Black Swan*, which propelled Natalie into the stratosphere.)

Peter Bradshaw of *The Guardian* was amused and gave it some credit for entertainment value, saying it was a 'flashy, silly, undeniably entertaining Tudor romp ... It is absurd yet enjoyable, and playing fast and loose with English history is a refreshing alternative to slow and tight solemnity; the effect is genial, even mildly subversive ... It is ridiculous, but imagined with humour and gusto: a very diverting gallop through the heritage landscape.'

Sukhdev Sandhu of *The Telegraph* was considerably more

reserved, writing, 'This is a film for people who prefer their costume dramas to gallop along at a merry old pace rather than get bogged down in historical detail ... Mining relatively familiar material here, and dramatising highly dubious scenarios, [Peter Morgan] is unable to make the set-pieces seem revelatory or tart ... In the end, *The Other Boleyn Girl* is more anodyne than it has any right to be. It can't decide whether to be serious or comic. It promises an erotic charge that it never carries off, inducing dismissive laughs from the audience for its soft-focus love scenes soundtracked by swooning violins. It is tasteful, but unappetising.'

In the United States the critical reaction was much sharper. Manohla Dargis of *The New York Times* was extremely scathing and described it as 'more slog than romp ... oddly plotted and frantically paced pastiche ... The film is both underwritten and over-edited. Many of the scenes seem to have been whittled down to the nub, which at times turns it into a succession of wordless gestures and poses. Given the generally risible dialogue, this isn't a bad thing.'

And Peter Travers of *Rolling Stone* wrote, 'The film moves in frustrating herks and jerks. What works is the combustible teaming of Natalie Portman and Scarlett Johansson, who give the Boleyn hotties a tough core of intelligence and wit, swinging the film's sixteenth-century proto-feminist issues handily into this one.'

The film was in fact notable for something else. While Eddie played Mary's second husband, her first, William Carey, was played by Benedict Cumberbatch. He and Eddie were

Above left: A fresh-faced Eddie poses with Emily Bromfield at the afterparty following the West End transfer of *The Goat, or Who Is Sylvia?* in April 2004.

Above right: Sharing a joke with Matt Damon at the world premiere of *The Good Shepherd* at the Ziegfeld Theatre in New York in December 2006.

Below: Fit for a queen: (*left to right*) Rhys Ifans, Eddie, Geoffrey Rush and Shekhar Kapur attend the *Elizabeth: The Golden Age* premiere in London's Leicester Square in 2007.

Above: Eddie and his co-star Alfred Molina take a bow on the opening night of the Broadway production of *Red* on 1 April 2010.

Below left: Posing with Michelle Williams at Dior's party for the Weinstein Company's premiere of *My Week With Marilyn* in New York in October, 2011.

Below right: At the London premiere of the film with stars Emma Watson and Kenneth Branagh.

Above left: Backstage at the Burberry Autumn Winter Womenswear Show with super-model-turned-actress Cara Delevingne during London Fashion Week in February 2012.

Above right: With his beautiful co-star Felicity Jones at the premiere of *The Theory of Everything* in Beverly Hills in October 2014.

Below left: Stephen Hawking attended the UK premiere of the film in December 2014. When Eddie triumphed at the Oscars for his role as Hawking, he dedicated his win to Stephen and his family.

Below right: A stunned Eddie accepts his Oscar from Cate Blanchett. He went on to say that he was recovering from the excitement of seeing her – 'an exceptional actor'.

Above: Eddie poses on the red carpet with his wife Hannah Bagshawe. The couple married in December 2014 in a 'winter wonderland'-inspired ceremony at Somerset's Babington House.

Below left: Pictured with fellow actor Mila Kunis at the Hollywood premiere of *Jupiter Ascending* in February 2015.

Below right: Caught on camera at a press meeting for the film *The Danish Girl* with the director Tom Hooper and co-star Alicia Vikander in March 2015.

All images © Getty Images

to merit frequent comparisons throughout the next stages of their careers, given their similarly privileged backgrounds and the fact that they were both to emerge as two of the leading actors of their generation. However, at that stage, in 2008, Benedict had the edge, as his career was about to go into overdrive. Eddie, on the other hand, while solidly employed and with a growing reputation, was still going to have to wait.

Not that he had much time on his hands. Still in period drama, Eddie went straight into a four-part television dramatisation of Thomas Hardy's tragic novel *Tess of the D'Urbervilles*. This told the story of Tess Durbeyfield, a poor country girl who discovers she is distantly related to the rich but villainous Alec D'Urberville. Her parents send her into his household in a bid to better her circumstances but she takes a strong dislike to him and rebuffs him, which ultimately results in his raping her. She falls pregnant and returns to her parents' home, just another disgraced young woman, but her baby dies and she eventually meets and marries the handsome Angel Clare.

Angel had been unaware of her past, however, and when he finds out what had happened, he abandons her and goes off to Brazil, leaving her in abject poverty. This caused some commotion when the book first came out in the nineteenth century, as the revelation comes about because Angel confesses to Tess that he had previously had a brief affair with an older woman in London. Thinking this means he will understand, Tess tells him about her own experiences.

Angel is most certainly not sympathetic, thus highlighting the different standards by which men and women were judged. Angel's actions drive her back into the arms of Alec, where she becomes a hardened courtesan, until Angel – by then penitent and aware he had greatly wronged her – returns to England and tries to reclaim her. Given that she had become Alec's mistress, this is impossible until Tess, driven to despair, stabs him to death. She and Angel run away and spend a few happy days together, until inevitably the police come for her. She asks Angel to take care of her sister Liza-Lu by marrying her after her inevitable execution; the novel closes with Angel and Liza-Lu watching as a black flag is raised, signalling her execution, and finally leave, hand in hand. While it is one of the masterpieces of English literature, a bundle of laughs it is not.

It was something of a departure for Eddie, as this was in many ways his first shot at the role of romantic hero, albeit a very flawed one. On British television, in particular, this kind of part can catapult an actor into stardom: from Colin Firth playing Darcy in *Pride and Prejudice* to Aidan Turner in *Poldark*, the handsome hero of a period drama can find himself becoming a very big star overnight. But while Eddie looked as good in period dress as anyone, that didn't happen for him – perhaps the tale was just too dark.

The production attracted the usual flurry of big names. Tess was played by Gemma Arterton, the treacherous Alec was played by Hans Matheson and other cast members included: Ruth Jones, Anna Massey and Kenneth Cranham.

The series was written by David Nicholls, who was about to become famous for a modern-day weepie novel, *One Day*.

The BBC was very excited about the new production. It put out a press release in which executive producer Kate Harwood said, 'Arguably Thomas Hardy is the most neglected of our great literary authors, so I'm delighted to announce this new BBC adaptation of his renowned classic tale of *Tess Of The D'Urbervilles*. Hardy's novel explores love, betrayal and the emotional burden of secrets locked away at the heart of a passionate, loving relationship which, when unlocked, implode with heart-breaking consequences. David Nicholls's adaptation brings Hardy's tragic heroine, Tess, to life with verve, passion and sensitivity.'

Eddie, who thanks to his classical education would have already been familiar with the novel, was very enthusiastic about the project. 'I had a stronger emotional attachment to this script than anything else I've ever read,' he said in an interview put out on the BBC website, complete with a picture of him looking very fetching in a straw boater. 'I started reading the scripts and finished all of them within three hours. The character of Angel is liberal, a little bit out there for his time. He works at the Talbothay's dairy farm, to get some practical experience of agriculture as he hopes to buy a farm one day, rather than follow in his father's footsteps as a clergyman.

'When Angel is really tested, on their honeymoon night, Tess reveals she is not a virgin, he proves he's not at all liberal and can't forgive her. It shows, when confronted with reality, he reacts completely differently ... Also in this adaptation, Tess's purity and strength of character is very modern and we see a transformation from a girl to a woman. It highlights the difference to sex and relationships when it comes to men and women. Also the reality of life then, the day-in day-out toil with no respite, gives a real insight into those times.'

The other actors also had their take on their characters. Gemma said of Tess, 'I was attracted to the role because stripped down, it's such a basic story about love and missed opportunities, everyone can relate to it. It's also just brilliant, brilliant storytelling. [Tess is] a straightforward country girl, very pretty, but unaware of her beauty. Although people chip away at her life, she grows stronger, which is the incredible thing about her.'

And Hans said of Alec, 'Although Alec's actions are extreme, they're unconscious. So you have to understand him as a human being, as well as a villain ... [The story was] about the countryside ... [about] spring and the seasons and the descriptions of love.'

The drama was directed by David Blair, who showed commitment to the story and also clearly saw the full extent of Eddie's acting ability. 'Eddie has that quality that suggests there is always something in reserve,' he told *The Daily Telegraph*. 'He is very bright and he doesn't tell us everything about himself upfront, which makes him very interesting.'

David Nicholls had been familiar with the book for many years before he came to work on the adaptation. 'I first read Hardy as part of my A-level syllabus,' he wrote in *The Sunday Times* several years later, after Eddie had become really famous and when he was adapting another Hardy Novel, *Far from the Madding Crowd*. 'As a rather emotional, romantically inclined student, I was acutely susceptible to novels about doomed love, cruel fate and an unjust and hypocritical society, but even so I found *Tess of the D'Urbervilles* intensely moving. Over the course of that summer, I read *The Mayor of Casterbridge*, *Jude the Obscure* and *Madding Crowd* and loved them all. Years later, I had the pleasure of dramatising Tess for BBC One, with Gemma Arterton as the resilient but doomed heroine and an up-and-coming young actor called Eddie Redmayne as Angel Clare. That production was one of my happiest experiences.'

And the project had been one he was keen to tackle. 'It seemed to cry out for a new screen adaptation,' he said on another occasion, adding that Tess was 'an active, forceful, opinionated young working-class woman [not just a] passive victim.'

Filming took place in Gloucestershire and Wiltshire, as well as other locations such as Dorset, where the novel was set. Nicholls said, 'Any adaptation of Hardy has to capture the beauty of his nature writing without forgetting that this is a brutal, unforgiving landscape,' adding, 'the production should be beautiful but not "pretty"; it should be about characters in a landscape, not just the landscape.' It also made use of some very famous landmarks: 'Tess and Angel's farewell in the morning light at Stonehenge ... the most moving scene in English literature, so to be able to recreate it, at dawn, on location at the correct time of year, has been tremendously exciting,' Nicholls added.

The beautiful scenery created one almost unavoidable problem: it looked almost too good. England and indeed the pair of doomed lovers had never appeared lovelier, but back in the gritty nineteenth century, that would not have been the case. 'The main thing to say about *Tess of the D'Urbervilles* is that it looks lovely, which is the point of any costume drama: fidelity to Thomas Hardy's bleak world-view isn't going to shift overseas broadcast rights and DVDs; it's frocks and rolling countryside you want,' wrote Robert Hanks in *The Independent*. 'Possibly it's a bit too lovely. The opening scene of David Nicholls's adaptation had Tess and the other local maidens dancing around in their best frocks on a picturesque if inconvenient clifftop, wearing more gleaming white fabric than in a Persil advert.'

It was widely considered to have been an excellent production, with the two main characters wringing every ounce of pathos from the tragedy that they could. 'Thomas Hardy continues to pile on the misery until finally Tess breaks and is forced to sacrifice herself for the sake of her family,' is how David Chater in *The Times* puts it. '"These judgments come, and I am punished again – and again – and again," she says. "I do not deserve this." Nor does she. Hardy grants her a brief respite and then delivers his final knockout blow – only by then she is resigned to her fate. "It is too late for me now," she says. "I am already dead." The actors playing Angel and Tess (Eddie Redmayne and Gemma Arterton) go for broke and play the two doomed lovers with such intensity and conviction that the endgame is as harrowing as anything that Hardy could have wished for. Poor Tess.'

Mike Bradley of *The Observer* was similarly impressed. 'Following the death and burial of Tess's father, John Durbeyfield (Ian Puleston-Davies), the family are turned out of their house on account of Tess's "queer unions",' he wrote. 'They gather up their possessions and travel to the village once owned by the blighted D'Urbervilles. From here on, in the last episode of David Nicholls's masterful dramatisation of Hardy's classic, a series of dramatic events build to a not wholly unexpected conclusion. More memorable performances from Gemma Arterton as Tess and Eddie Redmayne as Angel: two young actors to watch.'

Of course, not everyone was so enchanted. Andrew Billen wrote a wickedly amusing review in *The Times*: 'Dressed in finery bought for her by the wicked Alec, her hair up where usually it lay over her shoulders, her fingernails for once burnished, Tess looked every inch the femme fatale, which indeed she was, having murdered Alec with the boarding house bread knife. Pure no more, she and Angel, her estranged but now won-back husband, had exceptional sex in one of the rather fine mansions the citizens of Wessex left unattended in those days. The lovenest was decorated with a large tapestry of what looked like the Garden of Eden. Expulsion was inevitable. Soon the doormat-crossed lovers were sharing a less comfortable bed at Stonehenge, whose slabs were also left unattended in those trusting days.'

But in the United States, where the production was shown as a two-parter, a much more emotional review was given by Mary McNamara in the *LA Times*. 'As those who have read the book or seen any of the film adaptations know, Tess is not for the weak of heart,' she wrote. 'It is, in virtually any incarnation, what one might call a sobfest. With a four-hour run time, a lead actress who never looks as lovely as when she is blinking back tears and camera work that continually offers gorgeous vistas you know will only turn eventually to ash, this BBC version should be approached with caution.'

As should a great deal of Hardy. But Eddie had now shown that he could play a romantic lead – and one who needed to carry the production at that. He had achieved the next step up on the ladder of fame: not a household name, but a face that was becoming increasingly familiar. And still the work was flowing in.

Next up was a film called *Powder Blue*, written and directed by Timothy Linh Bui, which was to turn out to be Patrick Swayze's last film. Given that Swayze had been a massive star in his day, it was a shame that his swansong hadn't been better. However, it boasted some very big names, which led some critics to speculate on why they could possibly have decided to become involved with such mediocre fare. This wasn't a big Hollywood number and it only got a very limited release in movie theatres, ending up achieving its main viewership via DVD. Any film that pretty much goes straight to DVD can be judged on that fact alone and this film was no exception. It revolved around an ensemble cast playing characters who met by chance in Los Angeles on Christmas Eve: Swayze played Velvet Larry, who owned a strip club, and Jessica Biel was Rose-Johnny, who danced in said club. She also had a young son in a coma. Eddie was Qwerty Doolittle, a mortician who was in love with her, and elsewhere Kris Kristofferson was Randall, the head of a corporate crime organisation who was trying to stop Jack Doheny (Ray Liotta) from wreaking vengeance on his co-workers. Jack would also turn out to be the estranged father of Rose-Johnny and as if this were not enough, Charlie (Forest Whitaker, who was also one of the film's producers) was a suicidal ex-priest sharing a bond with Lexus (Alejandro Romero), a transvestite prostitute. There was so much for the viewer to deal with – too much trauma, too much tragedy – that it became nonsensical and it had the ultimate effect of leaving the audience totally unmoved. Or worse, laughing.

As before, it was no one's finest hour and the film was widely panned. The critics were not kind: Melissa Anderson, writing in *Variety*, set the tone when she opined: 'Another Los Angeles-set multistrand drama "Crash"-es and burns in Powder Blue, Timothy Linh Bui's tale of the intersecting paths of a stripper, an ex-priest, an ex-con and a mortician. The heartstring-pulling contrivances of the film, set during Christmastime, go way over the top, and include a child in a coma, a missing dog and a dying man determined to make amends. Those drawn by name cast members such as Jessica Biel ... or Patrick Swayze ... will rep the main audience for this direct-to-DVD release.' Ouch. But that was pretty much what an awful lot of other people felt.

Vadim Rizov in *Village Voice* also disliked it intensely and, in his case, singled Eddie out for a mauling, although he appeared to be as annoyed with the character's name as its portrayal: 'Timothy Linh Bui's second feature is one of those solipsistic, overwrought only-in-L.A. projects, in which four strangers are alone in the big city, etc. Besides Biel and Liotta, there's also Forest Whitaker and – rock-bottom – Eddie Redmayne as Qwerty Doolittle, presumably named by people with strong feelings about keyboard layout.' (Qwerty is the spelling of the left-hand side of the top line of letters on a keyboard.)

Jason McKiernan on *Filmcritic.com* denounced it as 'an embarrassing display of directorial exploitation and a waste of acting goodwill,' but Kam Williams on *Sly Fox* was a little kinder. 'A serendipitous erotic thriller reminiscent of *Crash* in the way that lots of Angelenos' lives intersect serendipitously, except that here the characters have a seedy strip club in common instead of car accidents,' he wrote. Nevertheless, you couldn't help but notice that his was very much a minority view.

All in all, it was one to chalk up to experience, but it showed that Eddie was not afraid to take risks.

CHAPTER SEVEN

ART FOR ART'S SAKE

By 2009 Eddie's professional reputation was soaring but it was taking its toll on his personal life. His relationship with Tara was coming to an end and he was about to discover one downside of fame: being linked to practically every woman he was photographed with – and, given that he was not only an actor but also a model, there were quite a few of them. Not yet aware quite what was about to hit him on the rumour mill, he laughed it all off. 'Ladies and babies, and mortgages, for that matter, can all wait,' he said brightly. 'Acting has done a strange thing to me, though. I often sit there, thinking, "I love this, but I wouldn't put my daughter on the stage."'

'Stage' was the right word, because Eddie was returning to theatre, his first love, in a play that could not have been more suitable for him, considering his art history background. The play, by the US playwright John Logan was called *Red*; directed by Michael Grandage and first staged at the Donmar Warehouse in December 2009, it was about the great artist Mark Rothko. Alfred Molina starred as Rothko, while Eddie was his fictional assistant Ken and it was to be a resounding triumph.

Its success could have been quite surprising, because in a way *Red* was a very cerebral piece: a debate on the nature of art that was simply a two-parter between the two leads. Set in Rothko's studio in 1958–9, the premise is that the great man had been asked to create a series of murals for the very upmarket Four Seasons restaurant. Ken is on hand to help, but as he mixes the paints, makes the frames and prepares the canvases, he starts to challenge Rothko on his theories about art and, above all, the reason why he is doing commercial work for the restaurant ('the flashiest mural commission since the Sistine Chapel'). By the end Rothko has had a huge change of heart and decides that he will return the money and not do the work for the restaurant after all. The play was based on reality and in real life Rothko kept the work secret for years before making a gift on nine canvases to the Tate.

Eddie was in his element. He had the chance to talk not only about acting, but also about art, and he did so with some considerable degree of enthusiasm, stoking up further interest in both him and the play when his colour blindness came to light. For a start, he'd be mixing paints on stage.

'We will see how qualified I am to do that,' he told *The Daily Telegraph*. 'Hopefully it won't be too embarrassing. It will be fun for the audience to watch us crush pigments, cook paints and prime canvases. That'll be luscious. I imagine the Donmar is going to stink of white spirit for the next three months.'

Eddie was enthusiastic about every project in which he became involved but this one even more so than usual. 'I don't want to be irritating about it, but this is the dream job for me,' he continued. 'There is also a feeling in the play that Rothko is rallying against the pop artists. My character represents a new generation of artists dealing with mass media, advertising and the commercialism of art. Rothko resented everything that represented, and by taking on the commercial commission for the Seagram Building he felt, in some way, as though he were selling out.'

Eddie wasn't the only one to think this was his ideal job: director Michael Grandage also thought Eddie was perfect for the role, offering it to him just two weeks after he'd seen the script for the first time. 'I knew immediately that he was right for the role,' he told *The Daily Telegraph*. 'And Eddie, rather sweetly, accepted the part as quickly as I offered it to him.'

To date, this is the theatrical performance for which Eddie is probably most famous. He was still a young and inexperienced actor in many ways, but he totally held his own against the more experienced Molina. Throughout the play he passionately argued the case for art for art's sake (or

103

an approximation of that at any rate), his character growing in stature as he forced Rothko to confront the reality that he was reducing the production of great art to the state of a commercial transaction (although in fairness, Rothko certainly wouldn't have been the first person to have done that). It was exactly the sort of part that would appeal to any young actor, but all the more so when that actor had some experience of the art world, as Eddie did.

Audiences loved it and Eddie got the chance to appear abroad, too. The play was to transfer from the independent Donmar Warehouse to the West End and from there on to Broadway. It had passion and it had power, and it argued that some things in life are more important than just money. It also confirmed Eddie as far more than just another pretty boy, part of a new generation of Old Etonian actors; so far, his past choices of theatrical roles had been both brave and experimental, but his talent could almost have been overlooked because of their sheer strangeness. In this case, however, the full extent of his abilities was not obvious and it was clear that theatregoers – like television viewers and film enthusiasts – were beginning to see the emergence of a major new star.

The critical response varied enormously: some of it was well-nigh ecstatic and some somewhat muted, although Eddie and Molina came in for a great deal of praise. *The Daily Telegraph*, for example, was not impressed: 'Unfortunately the play, which uses the tired device of a new assistant arriving at the studio, so that Rothko can bang on about his art, life and opinions, is far less riveting than the paintings themselves, superbly re-created in Christopher Oram's wonderful design,' it said.

Bloomberg too was unimpressed: 'Playwright John Logan portrays Rothko (1903–1970) as a monster of selfishness, pretension and jaw-aching verbosity. The writing is so slow and lacking in dramatic conflict that it can't help tainting the subject … Alfred Molina does his best to round out the flat role of Rothko. He varies the tone of the long monologues with occasional notes of despair, anger and sardonic dryness.'

The Times did, however, praise Molina: 'Moreover, Molina's blunt, bitter, baleful Rothko is able to communicate a ferocious pessimism to Eddie Redmayne's Ken, the aspiring artist who becomes his assistant and much misused lackey. Indeed, he rages unforgettably against the dying of the light as it is represented by those paintings in which rectangles of black overwhelm the reds he saw as symbolising life.'

Variety was far more impressed: 'Audiences expecting neat life lessons about artists or a simple-minded attack upon/ salute to abstract art will be disappointed. *Red* is far more ambitious, which makes its success all the more satisfying. That its central character is such a key figure in American culture can only hasten the play's arrival in the U.S.'

The Independent showered praise on Eddie: 'As Ken, Eddie Redmayne gives further proof that he looks set to become the Mark Rylance of his generation. (Praise can't reach higher than that.) Here, he plays an initially meek assistant who is goaded into stingingly sarcastic arias of repudiation of Rothko and his values. Lean and whippety, Redmayne combines highly strung intelligence with the knack of seeming to have one layer of skin and one keenly apprehensive sense more than other people. So he's thrilling to watch as, heart clearly thumping and adrenal system in overdrive, his Ken inveighs against Rothko's over-investment in the expressive properties of colour.' And so did Michael Billington in *The Guardian*: 'Alfred Molina, with his large frame and beetling eyebrows, has exactly the fierce intensity of an artist whose paintings were a dynamic battle between Apollo and Dionysus, and who once said that he saw art as a means of direct access to the "wild terror and suffering" at the heart of human existence. And Eddie Redmayne as Ken moves with total ease from nervous pupil to combative antagonist. It's a measure of the play's success that it makes you want to rush out and renew acquaintance with Rothko's work.'

WhatsOnStage Review was more enthusiastic still: 'Two reasons to rejoice at the Donmar: a really good play about art (Art is about friendship, not art), something of a rarity, by an unknown writer, John Logan, and the overdue return to the stage of Alfred Molina as the gloomy dauber Mark Rothko.'

The Stage said, 'But there is no doubting the brilliance of Alfred Molina's performance which inhabits Rothko's despair almost as if he is trapped inside one of the dark black lines of a Seagram mural.'

And *London Theatre Guide* opined: 'Alfred Molina plays

the artist as a volatile, self-obsessed man whose mood swings from one extreme to the other quicker than his assistant can hand him a paintbrush. He ably depicts the central paradox of Rothko and perhaps any artist; that he is not painting to gain public approval, to be liked, to be commercial, and yet he must be commercial to make a living.'

Most of the reviews made it clear that this had been a hugely important production, showcasing both an established talent and an up-and-coming one (this time, mercifully, in a role that was unlikely to upset his parents). It went on to win its fair share of awards which, perhaps more surprisingly, came from the United States, where the play was set and where it possibly found a more receptive audience. The play ran there for fifteen weeks on Broadway in 2010.

It was during the Tony Awards in 2010 that the play received the critical acclaim so many thought was its due. It was nominated for a total of seven Tony Awards, of which it won six, including: Best Play, Best Featured Actor in a Play (Eddie), Best Direction of a Play (Michael Grandage), Best Scenic Design of a Play (Christopher Oram), Best Lighting Design of a Play (Neil Austin) and Best Sound Design of a Play (Adam Cork). Alfred was also nominated for the Tony Award for Best Actor in a Play for his role as Mark Rothko, and in total it received the most wins out of any other production that season.

The play also won the Drama Desk Award for Outstanding Play, while Grandage and Austin were honoured with Drama Desk Awards for their work. In the grand scheme of things, it could be said to be one of Eddie's successes, which helped to promote his inexorable rise up the acting ladder, as it continued to introduce him to new audiences and showcase his talents to their full. The comparison to Mark Rylance was now an oft repeated one: no one was in any doubt that a major new talent had arrived.

That juggling of stage, screen and TV work didn't stop, though, and Eddie began preparing to star in his next film, *Glorious 39*. Directed by Stephen Poliakoff and with the usual host of big names that was coming to be expected in Eddie's films – Romola Garai, Bill Nighy, Julie Christie, Jeremy Northam, Christopher Lee, David Tennant, Hugh Bonneville and Jenny Agutter – the story was framed at the beginning and the end by scenes shot in the modern day but was mainly set in World War II and centred on the Keyes family, which was trying to maintain certain standards as chaos reigned all around. The focus of the story is Anne (referred to as 'Glorious'), an up-and-coming young actress and the eldest of the three Keyes children who, unlike the other two, had been adopted. She stumbles across information that reveals that her family, headed by Sir Alexander, an MP and World War I veteran, is involved in the movement to appease Hitler and the Nazis – a course of action recommended by some people at the time as the only way of saving Britain. Eddie played Ralph, Anne's brother, who was very much in on the plot. Ultimately, Anne is betrayed by everyone, including her father.

The film was set in Norfolk and mainly filmed there, with locations including the ruins of Castle Acre Priory,

Walsingham Abbey, Cley Marshes, Holkham Hall and Houghton Hall. Eddie was very similar in personality to the character he played (minus the treacherous details) but ironically found it a stretch to get into the role; 'Despite the fact that we were shooting the glorious summer of 1939 in freezing-cold Norfolk, it was a really wonderful shoot,' he told *The Daily Telegraph*. 'We lived the quintessential English dream in Burnham Market and I got to wear very high-waisted trousers, which Bill was jealous of. I don't want to give the story away, but it was a tricky part for me. The irony is that I found it most tricky because I was playing so close to type. I was playing a guy who had probably been to Cambridge, and probably been to Eton, yet I had to have dialect lessons. I couldn't believe I struggled with it. That messed with my head a bit.'

What Eddie had no personal experience of was the period itself, with Britain on the verge of war, a sense of foreboding and wildly differing views in the upper echelons of the establishment as to what the country should do next. 'What is essential in understanding the complexity of the piece is that there are no villains,' he observed in one interview. 'These are not stereotypes of people. They all believe that what they're doing and the reasons they're doing it are valid. They very much love each other as a family but there is a higher reason for all the work they're doing and that is that my father (sic) has fought in the Great War and has a strong memory of it as a massive generation in Britain at the time did.

'That was too violent a memory even to consider the idea of going back to it. And so my dad has fed me this piece of information and I absolutely believe that the idea of appeasing and preventing Great Britain from going into war was the right thing to do. That's what fills this piece because our manipulation of Anne and particularly my character's – he does love her. He keeps saying throughout the piece, "Just be an actress. It's what you do. Keep doing it," each time she volunteers something, but she doesn't listen.'

The film was clearly intended to be a tense thriller, but most critics agreed it didn't really live up to what it had set out to achieve. 'Stupendous turn from Romola Garai in the lead role but, while this sets up intrigue and atmosphere well, the plot devices creak audibly towards the end,' wrote Philip De Semlyen in *Empire* magazine. 'For all its sumptuous production design, Stephen Poliakoff's tale of glamorous toffs and treason is so laboured and slow that it's practically pensionable,' was how Wendy Ide described it in *The Times*. 'Prestigious and serious-minded, but it's still nonsense,' opined Nicholas Barber in *The Independent on Sunday*.

'Poliakoff's flaccid script and indulgent cut undermines a beautifully shot thriller with an excellent cast and original central idea,' was the verdict of Matt McNally of Film4. 'Unfortunately, Stephen Poliakoff's tale of wartime skulduggery should have stayed on paper. The sort you can flush. Tedious, overlong and laughably unconvincing, the only remarkable thing about it is Bill Nighy's performance. Specifically, how bad it is,' was instead the very harsh view of Elliott Noble of Sky Movies. Simon Reynolds of *Digital Spy* was even harsher, though: 'Trapped in a perilous zone between TV and cinema, this wartime conspiracy thriller ploughs through an improbable plot with all the urgency of a snail going through wet concrete,' he wrote.

Nevertheless, some people were a little kinder. 'A ripping, old-school conspiracy thriller,' said Xan Brooks in *The Guardian*. 'An enjoyable conspiracy thriller in the manner of John Frankenheimer's *Seven Days In May*,' concluded Philip French in *The Observer*. 'Poliakoff's conspiracy thriller about Hitler-pleasers and appalling aristos comes with all the bucolic loveliness you'd expect. But its biggest boost comes from Garai, whose fragile, hypnotic turn should make the actress a gong contender,' said Matt Mueller of *Total Film*. 'A political yarn – sometimes creepy, sometimes daft in the Hitchcockian vein,' wrote instead *Time Out*'s Dave Calhoun.

Eddie was nothing if not versatile, though, and so his next venture was something quite different. Billed as a horror film and in reality pure, old-fashioned hokum, *Black Death* was set in 1348, as the bubonic plague – black death – swept across England. It featured three veterans of *Games of Thrones* – Sean, Carice and Emun Elliott, who played Swire. Eddie played a young monk called Osmund, who asks his beloved Averill to travel with him to a remote village that is rumoured not to have been touched by the plague. Meanwhile, the feared knight Ulric (Sean Bean) has also heard about this village and commands Osmund to take him there, not least to find a necromancer who has been bringing people back to life. After a long journey involving all manner of unpleasantness, they arrive at the village, which has indeed been untouched and is led by a beautiful witch called Langiva (Carice van Houten). As Osmund is forced to choose between his faith and the village secrets, more horror ensues.

'I play a monk,' Eddie told one interviewer. 'A naughty monk with a girlfriend. He basically leads this group of soldiers, led by Sean Bean, to this village which is meant to be free from the plague and all this mysterious stuff starts happening like witchcraft.' He added, 'The director was Chris Smith, who is at the moment one of the greatest horror directors of England. I don't know anything about horror; I don't even enjoy horror, so for me it was a completely different challenge. I spent two to three months in a monk's outfit, in swamps in Germany, having the shit beaten out of me by Sean Bean. Was it fun? I dunno, but it was interesting …What happened is that the day before I was going to film it, I got a call from my agent saying that they wanted to shave my head. But because I was going straight on to *Pillars of the Earth* [of which more in the next chapter], in which the only feature that's really important in my character is that he has big red flaming hair, I wouldn't be able to do the job. So I had a fake tonsure which was so funny.'

As the film-makers were unable to find funding in the UK, this ended up as a German production; Jens Meurer of Egoli Tossell Films was the producer and filming took place at Blankenburg Castle, Castle Querfurt and Zehdenick,

Brandenburg in the state of Saxony-Anhalt. It was director Christopher Smith's second time making a film in Germany and he had a very clear vision of what he wanted to do. 'It's a "medieval guys on a mission" movie,' he commented. 'The period of the black death – what's fantastical and rich about that period? I said, "What if we took a realistic approach?" The people of the time believe the plague was sent by God to punish them for their sins, or by the Devil to torment them. I wanted to find out what the characters felt and posit them on a journey of "is it real? Or is it not real?" What would a necromancer be like if he existed? We added this fundamentalist knight, so it touches on fundamentalism. It's a super dark film but it's exciting. It's like a dark parable about how things haven't really moved on in the last 600 years.'

The film showed at the Fantasia Film Festival, which put out the following publicity blurb: 'Riveting and gasp-inducingly violent, brought to life with a solid cast that includes David Warner and Carice van Houten, BLACK DEATH is an atmospheric nightmare shrieking with horrors both physical and philosophical. It's a fascinating morality play that frequently shifts concepts of right and wrong as good characters do inexcusable things, bad characters do good, acts of violence are at once justifiable and indefensible, and ideals give way to instinct, then back again. You will regularly be shifting allegiances with characters you think you like or loathe, and once situations spiral out into full-on fury, you'll barely know which way is up. And that's when the blood really begins to flow. Smith's dependably intelligent directorial flair gives the film an earthy, personal feel, making the hellish proceedings all the more compelling.'

Critical opinion was sharply divided on this one, and although it didn't make that much of an impact overall, some loved it. There were quite a few comparisons to that great classic horror *The Wicker Man* which, like *Black Death*, featured a pagan community that was not exactly all that it seemed. 'Smith springs a savage battle of creeds on us with flinty assurance, engaging smartly with the tradition of cultish classics in this field, particularly Michael Reeves's immortal Witchfinder General. The coda to this grisly fable sends you out spooked and impressed – it's strong meat, and it works,' wrote Tim Robey in *The Daily Telegraph*, who also referred to the viewer 'nervously scanning the background for large-scale wicker-work.'

Jeanette Catsoulis in *The New York Times* was also a fan: 'With old-fashioned style and old-school effects – you can feel the weight of the broadswords and the crunchy resistance of every hacked head – "Black Death" takes Dark Ages drama to the limits of moral ambivalence. Here, excessive piety and rampant paganism are equally malevolent forces, the film's baleful view of human nature mirrored in Sebastian Edschmid's swampy photography. As is emphasized in a nicely consistent coda, the Lord's side and the right side are not necessarily one and the same.'

There were plenty of other good reviews; for example, Lou Lumenick wrote in the *New York Post*, 'Though deadly serious, Christopher Smith's European-made bubonic-plague melodrama provides good value with lots of blood and guts, as well as a solid cast.' Then again, Matt Joseph opened in *We Got This Covered* with: 'In *Black Death*, Christopher Smith effectively creates a creepy and unsettling atmosphere with great production values. He shows lots of potential as a director and I'm looking forward to seeing what he does next.' And James Luxford in *The National* commented, 'Smith's excellent, tension-building style is complemented from powerful performances from broadsword specialist Bean and Redmayne.' But not everyone took such a positive view.

In *The Guardian*, Alex von Tunzelmann hated it and took it apart bit by bit, citing numerous historical inaccuracies along the way. 'Nevertheless, it's all been a bit much for Osmund,' he says after listing where the film has been going wrong. 'He ends up galloping round the country burning random women at the stake to make himself feel better. At this point the film changes tack from *The Wicker Man to Witchfinder General*, which is correctly set in the real English witch craze of the 1640s. In these closing scenes, Osmund's tonsure has grown back. That doesn't entirely convey that he would have had to wait almost 300 years to become a freelance witch-hunter.'

Another take-down came from Kofi Outlaw at *Screen Rant*. 'It's almost as though screenwriter Dario Poloni had no idea that metaphor, symbolism, and subtlety are the earmarks of quality writing. Every single idea or theme presented in *Black Death* is just spouted out in dialogue so overt and unsophisticated that it had me burying my face in embarrassment for the person who wrote it ... We're basically treated to arguments we've heard between skeptics and believers a hundred times before, dressed up in chain mail and cheap Medieval costuming for no real purpose.'

It's not a film that Eddie talks about a great deal and it has certainly not notched up a reputation similar to the one of *The Wicker Man*, to which it is so often compared. But it didn't do his reputation any harm either, as it showed that he looked good in a monk's outfit and, once again, displayed his range.

CHAPTER EIGHT

GOING MEDIEVAL

Eddie was almost constantly in work by this point and his next role was to be part of an epic, with famous faces filling every role – and although it was on television, it was considerably more high profile than some of the films he had made to date. *The Pillars of the Earth* started life as a novel by Ken Follett, first published in 1989. It described the construction of a cathedral in the twelfth century in the fictional town of Kingsbridge during the Anarchy, a period of lawlessness which encompassed a war between England and Normandy that raged from 1135 to 1154.

The book had been a great success and in 2010 the novel was adapted into an eight-part television series, shown in various countries including the UK, USA and Canada. The plot in brief ran thus: the succession to the throne has been in doubt since the *White Ship* sank, with Henry I's daughter and nephew both intent on grabbing the prize. Meanwhile, Philip (Matthew Macfadyen) is elected as prior, thanks to Archdeacon Waleran (Ian McShane). Lady Aliena of Shiring (Hayley Atwell) turns down William Hamleigh's (David Oakes) marriage proposal and he dismisses Tom Builder (Rufus Sewell) from working on his house, throwing the family into poverty. They go to live in the forest, where they meet Ellen (Natalia Wörner) and her son Jack, played by Eddie. After Tom's wife Agnes (Kate Dickie) dies in childbirth, the lot of them make their way to Shiring Castle, just as it is being attacked by the Hamleighs in revenge for Aliena turning William down.

The second episode sees Tom, Ellen and the children turning up at Kingsbridge Priory, where Jack sets fire to the church. This means a new cathedral will have to be built, something that Tom, his son Alfred (Liam Garrigan) and Jack embark upon. Elsewhere, Philip gets caught between Bishop Waleron and the Hamleighs' fight for Shiring Castle, at which point Ellen is accused of being a witch. William and his cohorts attack Aliena and her brother Richard (Sam Claflin), and the Prior helps Ellen to escape.

The third episode opens with Aliena objecting to the fact that her father, Earl Bartholomew (Donald Sutherland) has been imprisoned, while Philip and William are at odds over access to stone in the Shiring quarry. Waleron and Regan (Sarah Parish) start plotting to have the cathedral moved from Kingsbridge to Shiring and Jack begins carving the stone of the new building. King Stephen (Tony Curran), Henry I's nephew, who is by then on the throne, visits but collapses in terror. The resourceful Aliena starts a fleece business to help her earn money to enable her brother to become a knight.

In episode four we have moved on four years; Henry's daughter, Princess Maud (Alison Pill), is besieged at Lincoln Castle and Robert of Gloucester (Matt Devere) is unable to come to her aid. William applies to have his father's earldom transferred to him and learns that he has a rival for the title; Regan has Waleran absolve William of all sins to help him get over his fear of hell. Stephen orders an assassin to kill Jack; Stephen and Maud, who are at war, each see the other's leader taken hostage and Philip confesses when Waleran admits to Maud that he betrayed Earl Bartholomew.

Episode five sees Waleran and Regan engineering a prisoner exchange in order to stay on the winning side, while Tom fails to build a bridge between Jack and Alfred. William attacks Kingsbridge to stop the fleece fair and damage Aliena's successful business, and the Hamleys and Philip gain rights to Shiring land.

Episode six has Richard returning from war to find his sister penniless; Alfred offers his services to Philip as master builder; Aliena is forced to choose between her love for Jack and her oath to her father. A year passes and Regan forces Waleran to speak to the king about William's delayed earldom. Waleran connives to remove Philip from his position and Aliena gives birth to Jack's son. She is turned out of the house by Alfred but is sheltered by Jack's mother and stepsister.

By episode seven (which featured a cameo from Ken Follett, the author of the original novel) we are in 1146, by which time Jack has learned how to create the cathedral 'filled with light' that Tom Builder wanted; Aliena, meanwhile, finds him by following the tracks of his carvings. Waleran offers Philip a new position in return for his allegiance, while Kingsbridge has regained its former wealth. Regan and William plan to attack Kingsbridge and are resisted by Richard, Jack and Philip.

In episode eight, the final part of the story, we have moved to 1156. Jack is totally preoccupied with the cathedral; Aliena, despite loathing him, is married to Alfred. Waleran and Alfred conspire against Jack and fail. Waleran's schemes are exposed, Jack and Aliena marry, and in 1170 the Cathedral is finished.

All in all, this was a big-budget international production which took about a year to put together in total, half of that filming, with a host of very famous names and a $40 million budget. Filmed in Austria and Hungary (Eddie was really beginning to see the world), it was backed by companies in Germany, Canada, the UK and the US – essentially a German-Canadian production in association with Ridley and Tony Scott, with a CGI cathedral inspired by the real life versions in Salisbury and Wells, the two buildings which inspired Ken to write the novel. Eddie was playing one of the main roles and it pushed his profile higher still.

The man himself was very excited about it all. 'This is the biggest project I've worked on in terms of the scale of the set,' he said. 'Three-quarters of a twelfth-century cathedral has been built in a field in Hungary. It's incredible. It is an amazing cast to be working with as well, including Hayley Atwell, Matthew Macfadyen, Donald Sutherland and Ian McShane. People who know *Pillars* from the novel are very passionate about it. The characters kind of get under their skin.'

As Eddie's profile was rising so fast, so was the amount of attention he was attracting. His usual charming self when talking about his character, he was in demand for interviews everywhere, not least because it is a while before Jack actually speaks – he is mute for the first episode – and so attention is centred on how he looked. Certain aspects of his appearance had been made more pronounced for the role to the extent that the audience's attention was immediately drawn to both his eyes and his hair, which had been dyed a vivid colour for the series. Eddie appeared quite amused by it all.

'His flaming red hair is quite a prominent part of the story and so there's these hilarious moments when you first come up to production and you have seven producers, directors, costume designers, and they're all standing there and they're not looking at your face, they're looking at your hair,' he told *Access Hollywood*. 'They're sort of frowning and you suddenly start taking your hair really personally. You're like "Oi! Don't be rude about my hair!"'

He did have a touch of the ginger himself, Eddie explained, but it had to be accentuated for this production. He took the teasing that went with it in very good part, as always, pointing out that not only was his hair reddish already, but that even his name was right for the role. 'I come from a family of brothers and there is definitely a redness in our hair, obviously in my name, but in this particular film, the character has bright ginger hair and I had to go through a huge hair-dyeing process. And all the stuff that I've read about it, it's sort of like "Eddie Red-Ma(y)ne is incredibly appropriate," "The ginger actor," and I'm like, "Noooo!" I spent all my life saying that I might have a mousey brown, with a bit of an auburn tinge, but I think I've given it all away with *Pillars* where I'm a full-on redhead.'

As ever, Eddie was keen to learn from the more experienced actors he was working with – 'When you're working with actors of Ian's calibre and Matthew Macfadyen … you try by osmosis to pick things up' – and he was enthusiastic about the challenges of a lengthy and complicated shoot. He was increasingly noticing what so many actors had found before him: when you're thrown together on location, intense friendships and relationships build up, as you're all in it together. And in this case they were also flung together in beautiful parts of the world, where there was lots to do in their spare time.

Eddie relished it all. 'The shoot was about six months,' he said. 'We shot it all in Hungary and then in Austria, and it was kind of dumbfounding. When you're working on something for that long there's an intimacy you get among friends, and it was a really eclectic cast of Brits, Canadians, and Germans, all based out of Hungary. There is a kind of summer-camp feel to it. You're all living in this wonderful city away from home and you develop close friendships. And it's rare that you get to work on something that everyone is deeply passionate about, and there's something about the story of *Pillars*. Most people who read [the novel], including Oprah [who selected it for her book club in 2007], have become so devoted to it as a story that we really wanted to serve the book and the story as well as we possibly could.'

With his Old-Etonian charm it is inconceivable that Eddie would ever have been less than enthusiastic about his fellow actors but he was even more effusive than usual here, providing a clue as to why it is almost impossible to find anyone to say a bad word about him, ever. And not only was he happy to praise his co-stars, but he also emphasised their career success – not something that is an absolute given in the acting community. That generosity of spirit was the true Eddie, though, and explained his lifelong popularity among friends and fellow actors.

'What was lovely is on the one hand, you have Sam Claflin, who plays Richard – who's now, like, the lead in the next *Pirates of the Caribbean* film, and Hayley Atwell [Aliena],' Eddie said. 'Sam had literally just left drama school and his career is just starting and is about to explode. And then you have Rufus [Sewell] and Matthew Macfadyen, who are wonderful British actors who have had these fantastic careers, and right up to Ian McShane and Donald [Sutherland]. We felt like at every level you had people to aspire to, or to learn from. There was a collective passion for it. We all really, really cared about the story, and the man helming it was a guy called Sergio Mimica-Gezzan, who was Spielberg's first for many years. He's such an ingenious talent. As you saw, the scale of it is so epic that to keep the momentum and the energy up for six months' worth of shooting every day was kind of formidable. So we were all behind him as well.'

And then there was the actual role. Eddie was used to challenging parts but in this case his life was made more difficult by the fact that, initially at least, he had to make an impact without actually speaking. That required a good deal of screen presence, although in the event he acquitted himself well. As usual, he put a great deal of thought into the character he was portraying. Another added challenge, of course, on top of the initial muteness, was that in this case he was portraying a character over a couple of decades' worth of story, which meant he had to change and develop as he got older.

'What I love about him – and actually why all the characters and the fabric of the piece works so well – is that they're all flawed human beings,' Eddie said. 'Jack is, maybe in some ways, the hero, but he does start mute. He's woven into the story gently as he's gaining confidence and passion, but he also retains his flaws throughout the piece, right up until the end. Whether it's his ambition for his art or his family commitment, I think that tempestuous or wild quality that he has from the outset is something that I wanted to [bring out]. So I suppose what attracted me to the part was that he wasn't your typical hero.'

In that, of course, he had a great deal in common with some of the characters that Eddie had played in the past. Indeed, it could be said that that was exactly the reason why Eddie made an impact so fast: he did not play the perfect, chiselled hero, but someone with what would today be called 'issues'. 'He was flawed, he was eccentric in some ways, and that was kind of amazing because it's rare that you get to read that sort of character,' Eddie commented. 'But also it was a massive challenge because, as I say, you were shooting for six months. At one in the morning you could be playing Jack when he's seventeen years old and then in the evening playing him when he's thirty-five years old. And you've got thousands of these scenes and you've got this wealth of material and you have to definitely be on your guard as to where, exactly, you are within the context of the story.' In the event he pulled it off, with some people lamenting that it took so long before he actually started speaking and others praising the characterisation he brought to the role.

Indeed, everyone did pretty well and the critics, on the whole, were quite enthusiastic. Series like these were all, to a certain extent, judged on their own merits, because you couldn't really compare a medieval epic with, say, *Coronation Street*, but on the mores accorded to this particular genre, the consensus was that everyone had done well. And quite a few of the critics pointed out that in many ways, this series – and others like it – were natural successors to the great Roman epics that had proven so popular.

'Hairy boots are the new sandals, mud is the new dust, a vast stone cathedral – the first to be built in the new gothic style with pointed arches and flying buttresses – is the new forum,' wrote Sam Wollaston in *The Guardian*. He was one of the critics to observe on this phenomenon, in a very good-humoured critique that praised the production while gently teasing it for the unavoidable complexities that the telling of such a tale involved. 'Because *The Pillars of the Earth*, a super-lavish adaptation of Ken Follett's epic historical novel, is the new *Rome* ... The cast is so vast that to begin with I have no idea who's who. Or what the hell is going on. It slowly becomes clear that pretty much everything is going on – politics and deceit, battles and power struggles, jealousy and revenge ... There's love, too, and lust, witchcraft, even some goodness and honour ... And the clearer it gets, the further in you get sucked.'

Michael Deacon, in *The Daily Telegraph*, wasn't quite as swept away and couldn't resist a few digs at what might be thought of as clichés – possibly unavoidable, given that if you were going to film a medieval epic, it was by necessity going to involve a lot of mud. 'Adapted from Ken Follett's novel, it's a tale of treachery, murder and the Church in twelfth-century England,' he wrote. 'Our hero is a penniless stonemason called Tom (Rufus Sewell), who is humble and pure of heart. You can tell 'e's 'umble an' pure of 'eart cos 'e speaks with a West Country accent, the way 'umble folks always do in 'istorical TV dramas. Much of Saturday's episode was devoted to political intrigue, with an ignoble nobleman (Stephen of Blois, played by Tony Curran) seizing the throne, and a priest (Waleran Bigod, played by Ian McShane) worming his way up the echelons of the Church. You knew the priest was a bad man because the costume department had made him dress as Professor Snape from the Harry Potter films.'

Alice Jones in *The Independent* found that it looked

promising and also drew the parallels with a Roman blockbuster. She was also one of the many who were vocal in their demands that Eddie should open his mouth and say something. 'More *Caligula* than *Cadfael*, this was historical drama in the mould of HBO's *Rome*,' she wrote. 'Racy elements – Witchcraft! Incest! Arson! Massive swords! – were thrown in at every possible opportunity. By the end of the relentlessly pacy opening double bill, all of these disparate elements had sort of fallen into place, ready for further bloody ructions and whispered intrigue ... Not allowing the excellent Eddie Redmayne to speak for two hours, though, was a criminal waste. Hopefully, he'll find his tongue for the remaining five episodes ... It's all rather cheesy and at times downright crude, but, *The X Factor* permitting, *The Pillars of the Earth* shows every sign of being as big a hit as *Rome* or *The Tudors*, which is surely what the programme-makers intended.'

And on the other side of the Atlantic, where the series was actually screened first, the response was generally very generous. Robert Lloyd of the *Los Angeles Times* opined, 'Starz, which has found success with its historical sword-and-sauciness series "Spartacus", updates the mix a millennium or so and raises the tone a bit with "The Pillars of the Earth," an eight-hour adaptation of Ken Follett's 1989 thousand-page novel of medieval England. Set mostly in and around the fictional town of Kingsbridge, which should not be confused with the actual British town of Kingsbridge, during a violent period of English history known as the Anarchy, which should not be confused with that song by the Sex Pistols, it is a tale of holy aspiration and earthly skullduggery, as various characters build monuments to God, fight for titles, feather their nests, fall in love, have sex in a cave, or invent the credit system and the flying buttress. Something, in other words, for everyone.'

And Mike Hale in *The New York Times* seemed to feel that everyone had done a satisfactory job. 'The tumultuous events in question take place in twelfth-century England during a period of civil war and church-and-state intrigue known as the Anarchy,' he wrote. '"Pillars," based on a thousand-page novel by Ken Follett, uses the building of the fictitious Kingsbridge Cathedral (modeled on the cathedrals of Wells and Salisbury) to tie together a story involving murdered royals, scheming clerics, master builders and shrewd businesswomen. That may sound high-toned, but rest assured that as boiled down for television, much of what's left are the good bits: incest, matricide, bloody self-flagellation, a weeping Madonna, sex in a dungeon, childbirth in a collapsing church and, in a particularly jaw-dropping moment, urination on a bishop.' In other words, it was a good deal of fun all round.

Concerns about his appearance aside, Eddie was thoroughly enjoying everything else that went with his work and growing reputation as an actor. Travel was one of the perks, because although he might have been busy, he was seeing so much of the globe these days. And for a culture vulture who was interested in all the arts, he was increasingly in his element, particularly with this production. 'But I do love the arts,' he told *Access Hollywood*. 'One of the great things about acting is you spend so much time living a manic life and kind of traveling all over the world. You get to go to wonderful galleries and extraordinary exhibits. Shooting *Pillars*, we spent a lot of time in Vienna and seeing some of the architecture, but also the art there was overwhelming.'

And something else that was increasingly beginning to happen was that he got recognised on the street. Until that point, he had been known mainly to the arthouse crowd – the small but committed number of theatre- and film-goers who made it their business to stay on top of what is going on in the avant-garde – but this was a role in a major television series that was being seen all over the world. However, Eddie was coping with it all pretty well.

'The hilarious thing that happens is that they recognise you … but recognise your face,' he said, of the increasing number of occasions when people did a double take when they saw him. 'And think: do I know you? And either they think you are a friend, alternatively what they do is they go: you're an actor. What have you been in? Which is a completely natural approach. You then have to go through your CV. And on the rare times that I have done that I go: "the Good Shepherd?" No. "The Other Boleyn girl?" Nah. "The Golden Age?" Definitely no. I haven't seen it. And you're like: "Do you want me to keep listing my CV to you?" Which is really humiliating.'

And had girls started to approach him? 'It really depends on where you are,' said Eddie. 'I went to a picture gallery recently and sat at a cafe. Schoolgirls came up to me and that was incredibly weird. When you're doing a play, people know where you are and then they'll come in. But it's not like I get sent knickers.'

As for who would be his ideal dinner party companions, he said, 'I was asked this question recently for a magazine … One would be Yves Klein who I'm a bit obsessed with. The other is a random Australian singer called Missy Higgins. Do you know Tom Sturridge? He's my best mate. We did a film together in Australia about four years ago [*Like Minds*] and we would just stroll around New Zealand in a car and there was a singer called Missy Higgins. A songwriter. And we can't work out whether she's straight or gay from her song lyrics. We became quite competitive over her. We genuinely believed that one day we would find her and ask her who she'd rather. So I'd have to invite Missy Higgins. Only four? I can't pick family. Who else … I'll throw in Rothko to see what they thought of each other and I've always been fascinated by Barbara Baekeland who's Julianne [Moore]'s character in *Savage Grace*, to see how she really was.'

But of course, the fact of the matter was that Eddie himself was becoming the sought-after dinner party companion, the person many would choose to hang out with if they could. To his enormous credit, though, he wasn't allowing it all to get to him and he hadn't gone on a big ego trip like so many of his fellow actors. For all his much-vaunted poshness, Eddie Redmayne was keeping it real.

CHAPTER NINE

FROM THE RIDICULOUS TO THE SUBLIME

Eddie was edging closer and closer to international stardom, but no one could claim that his next film was to represent his finest hour. *Hick*, a comedy-drama based on the novel of the same name by Andrea Portes, was directed by Derick Martini and premiered at the Toronto International Film Festival in September 2011. It saw Eddie return to the part of a somewhat disturbed character, in a road movie of sorts, in which thirteen-year-old Luli (Chloë Grace Moretz) runs away from her alcoholic parents, taking a revolver along with her. She hitches a ride to Las Vegas with a loner called Eddie (played by Eddie) and much drama ensues, including rape and murder, before Luli decides to go home again. Blake Lively and Alec Baldwin were also around to join in the fun.

The exceptionally generous Stephen Fitzpatrick, writing in *The Australian*, said, '*Hick* is worth the effort – and it does have some genuinely witty writing,' but critically speaking, he pretty much stood alone. Just about everyone else hated it – even those who were prepared to find something worthwhile in it all. 'It contains some effective performances, it does a good job of evoking bereft and empty landscapes, but what is it for? Has she learned anything? Have we?' asked Roger Ebert in the *Chicago Sun-Times*.

'Mostly plays like some creepy-perv fantasia looking for mileage from the mature-beyond-her-years presence of young star Chloë Grace Moretz,' opined Mark Olsen in the *Los Angeles Times*. And R. Kurt Osenlund wrote in *Slant Magazine*: 'It doesn't take long to gather the influences trickling through Derick Martini's *Hick*, an aimless tumbleweed of a road movie if ever there was one.'

'Ambles back and forth between tomfoolery and strained seriousness,' was the opinion of Drew Hunt in *Chicago Reader*, while Lou Lumenick in the *New York Post* snapped, 'A smarmy little road movie about a Southern teenage girl losing her innocence the hard way during the Reagan era.'

'Forced irony or klutziness? Too often that's the question you ask of *Hick*, which makes the answer all too clear,' sighed Rachel Saltz in *The New York Times* and Richard Haridy's opinion in Quickflix was: 'Derek Martini's second feature – after the competent *Lymelife* – is a confused mess of awkward tonal shifts and boring narrative tangents all encased in the discomforting shell of a Lolita fantasy.' All in all it was an effort better forgotten all round.

Eddie was now well-known enough for his personal life to become the subject of speculation. He was to be linked to a number of famous women over the next couple of years, including Carey Mulligan ('It's so sweet. They're both pretty crazy about each other,' confided a source). He was also about to embark on another film, which fared considerably better than his last.

My Week with Marilyn, the next project on the cards, was in fact altogether in a different league. Based on two books by Colin Clark – *The Prince, the Showgirl and Me* and *My Week with Marilyn* – the son of the art historian Lord Clark and younger brother of the Conservative politician Alan Clark, it charted events that took place in 1956 when Marilyn Monroe, at that point the biggest movie star in the world, came to London to make the film *The Prince and the Showgirl* with Laurence Olivier, who also directed it. The making of the film, which was released the following year, had not been an entirely happy experience, especially for the American star, who felt that she was not accorded the respect she deserved by Olivier.

Colin Clark, played by Eddie, had managed to get a minor role on the film and found himself working as a kind of assistant to Marilyn (Michelle Williams) and her husband, the playwright Arthur Miller (Dougray Scott), starting with finding them somewhere to live. Marilyn embarks upon work on the film but as her relationship with Olivier (Kenneth

Branagh) deteriorates, her behaviour becomes increasingly unstable. And when Miller returns to the States, she becomes more and more dependent on Colin, with the two of them spending a lot of time together, although the relationship is never actually consummated. It was, however, a deeply touching tale of a brief encounter between a megastar and an unknown – an ordinary moment for Marilyn in a very extraordinary life.

The film followed in the wake of *The King's Speech*, and while it never quite achieved that level of success, it was still a resounding triumph. Like *The King's Speech*, it tried to recreate an earlier Britain, very different from the one that exists today, and it was also peppered with appearances by half the senior thespians in the UK, with parts and cameos by the likes of Simon Russell Beale, Sir Derek Jacobi, Dominic Cooper and Zoë Wanamaker.

There had been intensive speculation about casting. Names in the frame for Marilyn included Scarlett Johansson, Kate Hudson and Amy Adams but the producers had always wanted Michelle and finally got her, managing to sign her up a full two years before filming actually began. She immersed herself in the role, watching endless Marilyn films, studying photographs, perfecting the walk with the help of a choreographer and, the supreme sacrifice for any actress, putting on a few pounds to play the part. 'As soon as I finished the script, I knew that I wanted to do it, and then I spent six months trying to talk myself out of it,' she told *American Vogue*. 'But I always knew that I never really had a choice.' She also added, 'I've started to believe that you get the piece of material that you were ready for.'

She had even grown up with a picture of Marilyn on the wall. 'I had one of her in a field of trees in Roxbury, Connecticut. She's wearing a white dress and she's barefoot and she's got her arms spread and she's laughing. There was just something about that image of her – so lovely and joyful and free. I've always thought of her as that woman-child, not an icon, which is probably why I let myself approach the role.'

The director Simon Curtis was delighted by his coup. 'Not only is she beautiful and brilliant, but she brings such intellect to her work along with an intuitive grasp of character, extraordinary depth of feeling, and a kind of innate glamour – I guess we call it star quality, don't we?' he told *Vogue*. 'For a director, it's the dream package. [The first time they met] was a wonderful, almost magical day. And I thought, My God, I pray she wants to do the part, because I can't imagine making it without her. We stopped somewhere on the way to dropping me off at the bus back to the city, and a fan asked for her autograph. Then the fan turned to me and said, "Is this your father?" That brought me back down to earth instantly.'

The role of Colin was also crucial to the film and although Eddie was very modest about the expectations he faced, he still had to beat off more than forty actors for the part, including James Jagger. 'It's a devilishly tricky part to find the right person for because Colin went to Eton, studied at Oxford and flew for the RAF,' producer David Parfitt told the *Daily Mail*. 'You also had to be able to believe that there was some sort of attraction between Clark and Monroe, whether or not anything came of it. The spark had to be there.' Given his obvious similarity to Colin, you could almost have said that Eddie was typecast – except that he wasn't, because he'd never played an Old Etonian before. He just happened to be one. And the Olivier role nearly went to Ralph Fiennes, but he had to pull out because he had to direct *Coriolanus*. Branagh, of course, turned out to be perfect for the part.

Eddie saw the similarities. 'I'm six years older than Colin but I'm an Old Etonian, too,' he told *The Guardian*. 'Weirdly, I found it just as challenging as playing the character I did in *Savage Grace*. What's been lovely is the variety of it all, and America has been very helpful for that. So much of our industry here is period drama, and given my background, that is what you slot into. But in America, because you're English, they send you off to everything because they can't bracket you. They'll go, "Can you play an adopted native American Indian? OK, go audition for it, why not?"'

But he was also experiencing the downside of his new life: 'I think all actors have a similar deal,' he remarked. 'You want some people who understand. Although it looks great – and is great – there are also shoddy moments when you feel really rotten, and when it's going well, you're not allowed to complain. Your actor friends will understand the nuances of a painful director, or the loneliness of being ... OK, in a beautiful hotel room somewhere exotic. But you're by yourself for six months, and you're thinking, "Oh God, I wish I could share it with someone." I'm trying to buy a house and set some sense of roots because otherwise you're constantly chasing one job after another, and you look back and you've had all these very extraordinary experiences with extraordinary people, but there's not a line of continuity to it.'

The central relationship – and the rows with Olivier, who was withering in his put-downs – was key to the film but there was more to it as well. Many people felt that the era in which the film was set was almost as interesting as the story itself. It was the mid-1950s, the end of the dreary post-war austerity period, and the 1960s were just around the corner. The old order was about to give way to the new. And the United Kingdom, for better or worse, was having to hand over the title of world superpower to the United States. Everything was changing and somehow that change came across in the film.

'At that time Olivier had become emblematic of a fading Britain,' director Simon Curtis told *The Daily Telegraph*. 'Marilyn was emblematic of an exciting, complicated new America. Arguably, 1956 is the year that Britain finally started to shake off the shadow of the Second World War. Rationing had only just ended. So for me, this is about Marilyn and her glamorous, colourful American entourage arriving in black-and-white England.'

The film was something of a risk for everyone involved in a way that many films were not, for the simple reason that it was based on real incidents, real people and recent history. Marilyn Monroe and Laurence Olivier were two of the most famous names in entertainment in the twentieth century and to bring them to life on screen, when there were still plenty of people around who remembered the whole thing, was always going to be chancy. It was particularly difficult for Michelle because she was setting herself up for a direct comparison with one of Hollywood's greatest ever sex symbols. Branagh, too, who had frequently been compared to Olivier himself, was also potentially in danger of attracting criticism, given Olivier's status as one of Britain's best actors. In reality, Branagh could more than cope with the comparison and, like everyone else involved, acquitted himself with honours. A film based completely on fiction could be judged simply on how it worked out, whereas this film had the added complication of being compared to the real thing. And it was so recent – Marilyn's husband in the period covered by this film, the playwright Arthur Miller, died in 2005.

Certainly, everyone involved was aware that there were issues involved in filming a story about Marilyn Monroe. She might have died more than half a century ago, at the very young age of thirty-six, but she was if anything more famous these days than ever. She is without a doubt one of the iconic faces of the twentieth century, instantly recognisable, and still the subject of fantasy, conspiracy theory and the rest. Everyone has opinions about her and preconceptions, and there were still fans so devoted that there was the possibility of upsetting them. It was not going to be an easy film to make.

Everyone involved knew it, too. 'Is there anyone more famous to write about?' was the film's screenwriter Adrian Hodges's take on it. He wanted to represent her as a whole person, not just a famous sex symbol. 'Princess Diana, possibly. Even people who don't know why they know Marilyn Monroe know her. That's how big she is in the culture. If you'd said to me one day I'd write a film about her, I'd have been amazed, because I wouldn't have known where to start ... [This is] a view of her as a woman of thirty, at a crossroads, still close enough to the person she'd been to have contact with reality. She was not quite the fading supernova. I liked the idea that this was before anything was inevitable for her. I felt the world could also use a generous view of Marilyn. The film isn't uncritical of her behaviour and it certainly doesn't give her a free pass. It's just that I think there are other things to say about someone who was once a complete person, not just this thing.'

Eddie had slightly different issues with his role: Colin was known, if at all, as the sibling of a more famous brother, but nonetheless, his relationship with Marilyn was central to the film. Strangely enough, Eddie and Colin actually had quite a bit in common – both attended Eton and Oxbridge, and both had art history in their background. Colin shows Marilyn around Eton and Windsor Castle in the film, both places that Eddie knew well. However, at other stages he said that in some ways this was a harder role for him to get into than some of his stranger outings, perhaps simply because he and Colin had much in common and, in a way, it wasn't necessary for him to stretch himself to get into this role. Unlike Eddie, though, Colin didn't have the sense of driving ambition that was keeping the young actor scaling increasingly challenging heights.

'There's a sense that Colin has come from a life of privilege,'

Eddie told *The Daily Telegraph*, 'but there was something idiosyncratic about him. He went to Eton, but while all his friends were hunting, shooting and fishing types, his father was an art historian – at a time when no one quite knew what a historian was. He was slightly embarrassed about it. At one point he became a zookeeper for six months, just because he wanted to. He had a rather glamorous background – with people like Olivier, Vivien Leigh and Margot Fonteyn visiting his parents' home for tea. So he came out of Eton and Oxford with tremendous confidence, but in need of an emotional education.'

Eddie was also aware that his character didn't quite attract the same high expectations as some of the others. 'In *My Week with Marilyn*, Michelle, Kenneth and Judi Dench [who played Dame Sybil Thorndike] were playing these icons but I didn't have to fulfill any public expectations,' he said. But he did have to make the character and the central relationship very convincing – a task he pulled off with aplomb.

Michelle Williams, meanwhile, had also been giving some thought to her role, confiding that she was 'desperate to do justice to an idol'. She also had quite a few issues to deal with, for not only had she been a Monroe fan in her youth, but her own former fiancé Heath Ledger, father of her daughter Matilda, had died after an overdose, just as Marilyn had done. 'I was so apprehensive, it was daunting living up to people's expectations as well as my own expectations,' she told the *Sunday Express*. 'There were so many connections and parallels for me in making this film. I was thirty when making the movie, the same age Marilyn was when she filmed *The Prince and the Showgirl*, the picture our film is based around. We filmed in the same studio at Pinewood where that movie was made. I had the same dressing room Marilyn had used and we also shot at the same house, Parkside, where she had stayed during filming.

'I watched all her films countless times, read her poems and letters, read a stack of books and viewed so many clips of her on YouTube. I had always been more interested in the private Marilyn, and the unguarded Marilyn. Even as a young girl, my primary concern wasn't with this larger than life personality smiling back from the wall but with what was going on underneath.' And did she, like the superstar before her, form any strong bonds with the people who worked on the shoot? 'The third assistant director on our movie [a reference to Colin Clark, the third director on Marilyn's movie] was a lovely young man who all the girls fancied but nothing happened between us. Maybe I should have done something though, it could have helped my performance!'

She was being too modest, as her performance was judged to be a great success. Michelle was also aware that behind the scenes there were greater issues going on than just the straightforward story, and she looked to address those. And on top of everything else, this had been for Marilyn a very troubled episode in an exceptionally troubling life. 'What Marilyn anticipated happening and what actually happened were two very different things and they created discord and unhappiness for her in England,' Michelle observed. 'She was expecting to go to London and make a movie with the most esteemed actor of the time and hoped it would bring her the respect that she deserved and craved. When she arrived she felt she was being mistreated and laughed at. Olivier sneered at her and didn't treat her with the kind of attention she was hoping for but when you watch the film now, you can see Marilyn wipes the floor with the rest of the cast. They are all very stiff, mannered and archaic but if she were making that movie today there is nothing about her performance that has gone out of fashion or faded. She is very real, very in the moment and so beautiful.'

The film had its world premiere on 9 October 2011 and turned up at various film festivals, including Cannes, the New York Film Festival, the Mill Valley Film Festival, Hamptons International, Chicago International, Wooburn Festival, the Philadelphia Film Festival, AFI Fest, the Rome Film Festival and the Dubai Film Festival. It was released in the UK on 25 November that year and, both commercially and critically, proved to be an enormous success.

Most of the critics liked it, showering the various cast members with praise, but they did voice some reservations, too. Although David Rooney from *The Hollywood Reporter* loved Michelle and Eddie, he did say, 'Fault lies with both Hodges' workmanlike script and Curtis' failure to excavate much psychological depth … [it was] superficial showbiz pageantry.'

Adam Green of *Vogue* remarked that it didn't have 'the high drama and urgency of a period piece like *The King's Speech*,' but added that Michelle played Marilyn 'with heartbreaking delicacy and precision without resorting to impersonation or cliché.'

Ronnie Scheib of *Variety* said it 'flits uneasily between arch drawing-room comedy and foreshadowed tragedy … [there is] no attention to spatial logic or rhythmic flow.' However, Rex Reed of the *New York Observer* called *My Week with Marilyn* 'pure perfection'.

The *Miami Herald*'s Rene Rodriguez stated, 'One of the chief pleasures of *My Week with Marilyn* – which should not be approached as anything other than fluffy entertainment – is watching Williams bring to life Monroe's inner demons and her movie-star allure with equal aplomb.'

Regina Weinreich of the *Huffington Post* called it a 'gem [the story] manages to convey so much of Marilyn, particularly her child-like vulnerability, her insecurity as an actress, her natural charm and talents. While we have seen Michelle Williams tap dance and heard her sing before – she was superb in last year's *Blue Valentine* – her moves and voice as Marilyn evoke the subject's understated, magnetic performances.' She also mentioned that the others were 'especially good'.

'Marilyn Monroe's presence could render even the blandest film watchable, so it's to Michelle Williams' credit that her depiction of the actress, singer and incomparable sex symbol has exactly that effect on this otherwise fairly rheumy-jointed period piece,' wrote Robbie Collin in *The Daily Telegraph*. 'Williams, lambent as ever, ably conveys the tension between Monroe's eyelid-fluttering public persona and the damaged woman behind it. She also has her voice and movements down pat, although after a significant amount of close study, I'm fairly certain it's with the help of some judicious padding.'

In contrast, Jenny McCartney in *Seven* magazine, part of *The Sunday Telegraph* newspaper, was not so keen. 'Much of the darker material that could have been fascinating – the emerging cracks in Marilyn's relationship with Miller, and his discomfort at being squeezed out by Strasberg – is simply thrown away,' she wrote. 'Great claims have been made for Williams's performance in this film, and I'm sorry I cannot fully echo them, except to say that she does well with an impossible brief. Monroe is an impersonator's dream and an actress's nightmare: anyone with a blonde wig and a painted vermilion pout can "do" Marilyn, but almost no one can slip into her soul.'

Having said that, *The New Yorker*'s David Denby loved it. 'In *My Week with Marilyn*, Williams makes the star come alive,' he remarked. 'She has Monroe's walk, the easy, swivelling neck, the face that responds to everything like a flower swaying in the breeze. Most important, she has the sexual sweetness and the hurt, lost look that shifts, in a flash, into resistance and tears.' It was 'charming and touching', he added.

In *Time*, Mary Pols said it was 'nothing more than a lively confection ... Williams locates a central truth, the contradictory allure of this utterly impossible woman – mercurial, vain, foolish, but also intelligent in some very primal way and achingly vulnerable.'

The great Roger Ebert felt that, 'What matters is the performance by Michelle Williams. She evokes so many Marilyns, public and private, real and make-believe. We didn't know Monroe, but we believe she must have been something like this. We're probably looking at one of this year's Oscar nominees.'

Manohla Dargis of *The New York Times* wasn't sure about Branagh but said that he made up for that with 'his crisp, at times clipped, enunciation and a physical performance that gives Olivier enough vitality so that when, early in, the character sweeps into his production office with his wife, Vivien Leigh (Julia Ormond), he dazzles Clark and jolts this slow-stirring movie awake. [Michelle] tries her best, and sometimes that's almost enough.'

Empire magazine's Angie Errigo gave *My Week with Marilyn* three out of five stars and observed: 'The "my week" chronicler in Simon Curtis' entertaining "no business like show" tale observes that Marilyn Monroe was a movie star who wanted to be a great actress, and Sir Laurence Olivier was a great actor who wanted to be a movie star. He ruefully concludes that *The Prince And The Showgirl*, a lack-much-lustre adaptation of Terence Rattigan's comedy *The Sleeping Prince*, would serve neither's purpose ... At moments hilarious and others touching, it's a sweet, slight affair, more pretty pageant than pithy biographical drama. Expect awards nominations to stack up for Williams and Branagh.' She was certainly right there.

The Wall Street Journal's Joe Morgenstern, however, was not impressed. 'When bad movies happen to good people, the first place to look for an explanation is the basic idea. That certainly applies to "My Week With Marilyn," a dubious idea done in by Adrian Hodges's shallow script and Simon Curtis's clumsy direction.'

'Williams makes the diva come alive with rare precision and although we have read everything there is to know about Monroe, watching Williams break down when she can't get her dialogues right, pose suggestively at a press conference and cling on to her husband's hand anxiously while watching rough cuts of the film, is surreal,' wrote Nishi Tiwari in *Rediff.com*. 'In the end, though, the only talking point of the film is Marilyn Monroe, not because the other actors, the script, the background score are bad, but because, as Olivier remarks while watching a rough cut of the film, "You forget everything else when she gets it right."'

Whatever anyone said, Michelle garnered no less than thirty-two nominations for her portrayal of the doomed star, quite a few of which she won. Kenneth Branagh didn't get quite so many but his name also cropped up repeatedly on award lists – sometimes also winning – and both were up for Academy Awards, although ultimately they didn't get them. Eddie was nominated for Rising Star Award at the Baftas and although he didn't win, he had clearly made his mark.

Even though some slightly negative reviews had appeared, the film was a huge success – one of Eddie's biggest to date. It is still remembered fondly and Eddie managed yet again to show that he could hold his own among some of the greatest members of the British acting community. But, as he had already done so often, he moved from one project to something totally different – and headed back to the stage.

CHAPTER TEN

REDMAYNIACS

The year was 2011 and over at the Donmar Warehouse, the scene of past successes for Eddie, the great Michael Grandage was coming to the end of a stratospherically successful ten-year reign as artistic director. During his time in the role, he had won just about every award going – including Tony, Olivier, Evening Standard, Critics' Circle and South Bank Awards – and had a sky-high reputation in the industry. And at that point he was thinking about what would be his last production for the theatre he had served so well.

In the event, he chose *Richard II*, one of Shakespeare's history plays. 'I did think of making *Lear* my last one, but I wanted *Richard II* because it's a young man's play,' he told *The Times*. 'My whole team – lighting, costumes, sound

– are young. I was in it at the National Youth Theatre – I was Bagot and Doug Hodge was Bolingbroke. He was always better.'

To play the title role, he chose Eddie. The two had previously worked together on *Red* and Grandage was sure that he would be right for the role: 'He has a weird combination of vulnerability and assurance,' he told *The Sunday Times*. 'The early scenes, where the king is under threat and becomes quite paranoid, are difficult to get right. It requires vanity and other negative qualities to be exposed, and actors care about how they appear.' But Eddie was prepared to take far more risks than many of his contemporaries – and compared to some of the oddballs he'd played in the past, Richard appeared comparatively normal. According to Eddie, the request, when it came, was not to be turned down: 'I'm going to say two words to you,' was how he recalled Grandage's phone call, 'and you have to say yes or no – Richard Two.' Eddie said yes.

This role was not an easy one to play; as one interviewer pointed out, Richard had twenty-seven per cent of the lines in the play – a phenomenal amount. 'I feel every ounce of that percentage, because it's taken me about six months to learn it, and I'm still not there,' Eddie told *The Sunday Times*. He described being up 'with the early-rising dog walkers and guys doing Buddhist-monk stuff, and I'm walking round talking to myself about the death of kings and what it is to be human.'

He added that friends told him he'd be perfect for the role, but when he read it, he found the character to be, 'arrogant and mildly irritating, then good with words – I'm the opposite of all that.'

Eddie was his usual, thoughtful self, seeing a parallel with the late Libyan dictator Colonel Gaddafi, who had recently been deposed and then found in circumstances that were a long way from his heyday: 'It's interesting that it still exists, this autonomy – until you hear he's been found in the sewers,' he commented. 'It's so simple, this idea of our constant striving for happiness. History reminds us of these questions being asked again and again.'

For the time being, he was enjoying the rehearsal process: 'I remember Alfred Molina saying that if he could just rehearse for the rest of his life, he'd be a happy man, and I totally agree. It's a wonderfully protective moment, when you feel you have all the freedom in the world to play. [Performance] is a different sort of enjoyment – almost like a long-distance runner. You have to pace your life for it. Plays are easier to choose than films. Even if *Richard II* is the worst production ever, and I'm hated by everyone in the cast and we get appalling reviews, I would still get something out of doing it each night. Whereas, with film, there are so many unknowables. You can have the hardest time on a film set and end up with something amazing.'

In the event, the production turned out to be another critical success. 'The two cousins are the core of the play: Redmayne's Richard is all eloquent, self-dramatising kingliness, yet beneath it lies the trapped, vacillating self-doubt of a man who knows that the role he was born to is beyond him,' wrote Libby Purves in *The Times*, continuing, 'Redmayne unpeels this pain, desperate self-delusion and vanity with great delicacy. Andrew Buchan as Bolingbroke is macho in warlike leather, his watchful stillness a tough secular contrast to Richard's theatrical posing. Once, the doomed King flickers in godly candlelight above while Bolingbroke is a dark, inescapable fact in the shadows below … It is a fitting final flourish to Grandage's Donmar years.'

Michael Billington in *The Guardian* was less impressed. 'Michael Grandage ends his dazzling tenure at the Donmar with a *Richard II* that has many virtues: clarity, speed, superb set and sound design,' he wrote. 'But the big question is whether Eddie Redmayne, currently hot in movies but inexperienced in Shakespeare, is ready for the title role. My feeling is that he has the temperament but not yet the technique to play the king.' In praising the production but not Eddie, Billington was being a little unusual, as normally when there were doubts over a play Eddie was in, the critical reaction was the other way around.

Nevertheless, Charles Spencer in *The Daily Telegraph* was much more complimentary. 'Michael Grandage ends his reign as artistic director of the Donmar Warehouse with a beautiful and moving production of a play about a king giving up his crown,' he reported. 'But whereas Richard II is a weak, vacillating figure who has abused his powers and brought his country to a state of shame, Grandage's rule has been both benign and packed with high achievement … Eddie

Redmayne confirms his status as one of the most exciting young actors in Britain today with his often mesmerising performance as Richard II. He is by turn grandiose, camp, maudlin and self-dramatising, and sometimes all of these things at once.'

Paul Taylor in *The Independent* also loved it. 'Eddie Redmayne's brilliant Richard is already installed on his throne as the audience take their seats for this marvellous farewell production by the Donmar's departing artistic director Michael Grandage,' he wrote. 'The air is laden with incense. The amber glow of candlelight picks out the vestiges of gilding on Richard Kent's wooden Gothic chamber of a set, their sparseness emblematic of an England fallen into neglect because of this monarch's spendthrift ways.

Resplendent in his ivory coat and crown, and cradling a sceptre, Richard gazes downwards wrapped in (and rapt by) the mystique of majesty. Redmayne must have to hold this pose, perfectly still, for half an hour.'

In *The Observer*, Susannah Clapp also commented on this endurance feat – an early sign perhaps of just how able Eddie was to use his own physicality to interpret a role. 'In Michael Grandage's production of *Richard II*, Eddie Redmayne, on stage as the audience enter, is enthroned by Richard Kent's design in tarnished gilt, among sneeze-inducing clouds of incense, the glow of candles and the peal of bells,' she described. 'He is so much part of this ornate ecclesiastical architecture, so entrenched in a stately establishment that it is hard to imagine he could ever be deposed. He thinks that too. Both cocky and tremulous, Redmayne captures perfectly the peculiar mixture in Richard of a man who feels born to rule but incapable of doing so; together he and Grandage unlock the difficulties of a play that is half-Henry-History, half Hamlet.'

Another fan was Tim Walker in *The Sunday Telegraph*. 'Each scene is composed with the meticulous care of an Old Master; he has managed to coax the usual sensitive performances out of his players; there is verve and purpose to the proceedings; and also there's the indefinable but irresistible sexiness about the enterprise that is his hallmark,' he wrote. 'His masterstroke turns out to be casting the twenty-nine-year-old Eddie Redmayne in the title role. Upon his youthful shoulders, the mantle of power weighs heavily from the beautifully realised opening scene, as he sits upon his throne, an elfin figure in a long white robe in a cloistered hall full of smells and bells. The actor – stiff, formal and full of self-importance at the outset – goes on to expose, layer by layer, the "gentleness" of his character in what turns out to be a performance of extraordinary emotional intelligence.'

Eddie's physicality was also the focus of Christopher Hart's comments in *The Sunday Times*. 'Eddie Redmayne, as the doomed king, smiles frequently, faintly, often inappropriately,' he reported. 'Add an awkward gait and hand movements, and a whole range of tics, twitches and mannerisms, and you have a Richard who seems more overtly unstable than he is usually played ... here the character is definitely on the way to somewhere else. He often has a vague, lost look, blinking rapidly when under stress, his mouth twisted aside, or staring at the ground around him, as if seeing things.'

Clearly then, apart from the odd exception, the play was attracting astonishing reviews, which described it as one of the must-see performances of the day, and generally catapulting Eddie even further into a career in which he was emerging as one of the most exciting new actors to appear for decades. With perfect timing there was a further frisson when it was announced that Mark Rylance was returning to the Globe to play *Richard III*: by this time he and Eddie had often been linked to each other even more and it seemed as if there was some kind of neat batting going on between the older actor and the younger, with comparisons so often made between the two.

By this time fame wasn't just bringing success, but material rewards, too, as he started to make some serious money. Eddie bought a flat in the Borough district of London, an area south of the river that had previously been run-down but had become very up-and-coming, containing the Tate Modern, the Globe Theatre and a well-known foodie market. He was enjoying life as a man about town. His fame had by then hit the point where he was accumulating his own devoted following, as for example, devotees of One Direction came to be known as Directioners. In Eddie's case they were Redmayniacs. This had a beneficial effect on the nation's literacy levels: some teenage girls confessed that while they didn't entirely understand the language, they went along to *Richard II* as they wanted to see Eddie. He had exactly the right appearance to be a teen pin-up: like almost every male recipient of the affections of teenage girls, Eddie had a slightly metrosexual air. They say teen idols have a delicate appearance because they appeal to girls at a time when they are moving away from childhood but are not yet fully mature.

He was also, for better or worse, becoming part of a social trend: it was around this time that people were beginning to notice quite how many Old Etonians seemed to be dominating stage and screen, and not all the comments were positive, especially when it turned out that Eddie had known Prince William. There was nothing Eddie or anyone else could do about it. Eton was bound to be a divisive subject in a country still acutely conscious of its class system: to some people it meant nothing and to others it rankled. That was just the way it was – or maybe it was worth debating. The tough-guy actor Ray Winstone, who was almost the polar opposite of Eddie in every way, came out in defence of this new breed of pretty posh boys. 'The new generation is a different class,' he said. 'It's going back to the old movie star look, which I haven't got. At least these kids have an education. This generation are more professional ... They understand literature much more than I did.'

Eddie was also still modelling and at the time working in a campaign for Burberry with the supermodel Karlie Kloss. When talking about her, Eddie was his usual droll self:

'That's the one my brothers started getting angry about,' he told *The Independent* in an interview at the beginning of 2012. 'They were, "All right, your life, stop it now." But this bombardment will slow down come February. The world will be sick of my face.' But that wasn't to be the case at all. The world was lapping Eddie up, constantly wanting more, and although there was some sneering from some quarters about his modelling, on the grounds that it was beneath a serious actor, the fact was that he was very sought-after in that world, too.

In fact Eddie was, incredibly, becoming conscious of his age: he had turned thirty, although he certainly didn't look it, and in an industry obsessed with youth, he was aware that he was a touch older than some of the competition. But although he was indisputably a very good-looking star player, there was more to him than that: he was a proper actor, not just a bimbo.

'An older actor said something to me many years ago: "The thing about you Ed, is that you look young for your age, so you'll have quite a good run of it until you're thirty and then it'll be interesting to see what happens." He didn't say it in a cruel way, but it's stuck in my mind,' he told *The Independent*. 'Fortunately, as a guy, you're luckier than the women, who have a really rough time of it. I have a lot of good actress girlfriends and when it gets to a movie level it's all about weight and producers sending you to boot camps and being really quite brusque with it. The guys get it, too: you have to buff up and there are gentle nudges. You didn't hire me for my pecs and, if you did, you fucked up! You hired me for my slightly off-kilter freckly appearance.'

And he was also aware of the futility of constantly trying to reach the highest peak. 'As an actor there's a lot of scrutiny and, even when you've had success, it becomes about sustaining that success,' he mused. 'A friend of mine described it as a peakless mountain. Even for De Niro there's Pacino and for Pacino there's De Niro. You're never going to reach the top, which is why it's important to take time out and be content with my luck to be working in three mediums with wonderful people. Just to say, "Right, good. It could be all downhill from here, but for now, it's lovely..."' These were wise words from such a young man.

In some ways *Richard II*, for which he won Best Shakespearean Performance at the Critics' Circle Theatre Awards, pushed Eddie into a different league in terms of fame and reputation. 'It's just the loveliest, loveliest thing that could have happened,' he said of winning in an interview with *The Independent*, which was especially sweet, as it came almost exactly ten years after he had played Viola in *Twelfth Night*. However, he was determined not to rest on his laurels, 'Because you never get it right. You never get it close to getting it right, you never get one line exactly how your notion of it should be. That's what's so exciting about theatre. Most actors hate watching their own films because all you can see is the glaring mistakes, your own tricks and ticks. But people often ask, how can you do the same play night after night for months on end and not get bored? And that's the reason. In theatre you always have the chance to try and fix what you did the night before.'

His career remained of paramount concern and so next up was a two-part adaptation of Sebastian Faulks's novel *Birdsong* (actually filmed before *Richard II*), originally published in 1993 and set in World War I. Directed by Philip Martin, Abi Morgan wrote the screenplay and the war scenes were filmed in Gyúró, Hungary. The story was told in flashback, with Stephen Wraysford (Eddie) recalling his wartime experiences, intermingled with his memories of an affair with the married Isabelle Azaire (Clémence Poésy, who was at that point best known for the role of Fleur Delacour in three of the *Harry Potter* films).

It was made by Working Title Films, which is the company responsible for some of the greatest successes of the British film industry in recent years, including *Four Weddings and a Funeral* and *Notting Hill*. They had held the rights to the novel for some years by this stage but decided this was the right time to act because Sebastian Faulks was enjoying a moment, as they say, since he had recently been invited to write a James Bond novel.

Eddie tackled the project with his usual enthusiasm. 'It was very odd on set, like two different films,' he said. 'We shot the war stuff first on this huge field outside Budapest with the most astounding rabbit-warren trenches, and it was incredibly hot and intense. But it was in Budapest and you had all the boys, this amazing collection of British actors like Matthew Goode and Thomas Turgoose, and – of course, they had days on and days off – so they were out on the lash in Budapest. I felt like the depressingly boring dad, living last night's action vicariously through them.

Then they all left after this hardcore six weeks, and these beautiful French actors arrived. It became this European period drama, so make-up off, mud off and suddenly into these starched ties. Philip [Martin] and I were like, "What's happening here?"'

Poésy was French and so perhaps didn't initially realise how deeply the British populace felt about *Birdsong*, but as she explored the story and the character she played, she also came to a greater understanding of the role. 'I think Isabelle tries – probably because she lacks something in her life, she's not very happy – to make everything very beautiful,' she told *The Sunday Telegraph*. 'She has a sense of aesthetic. There's a quote from the novel that says she gave off the sense of "having not merely dressed, but dressed up, as though in a costume that suited not the house but some other world she inhabited in her mind". That was a good note on [how to play] her. That kind of passion can all of a sudden make you feel as if you've had no idea who you were for a very long time. Isabelle experiences that, then experiences something else when she decides to go away with someone that she realises she doesn't know at all, once they're on their own and nothing is forbidden anymore.'

The original book contained some scenes in the modern day, which was one of the reasons why it had often been thought of as un-filmable – the structure was too complex to translate to the screen – but these had been jettisoned for the television production and it seemed to work.

'To say it's been a hard nut to crack is an understatement,' screenwriter Abi Morgan told *The Daily Telegraph*. 'It forced an impossible choice: whether we were going to make a war film or a love story, because there simply wasn't the time to do justice to both. [But] The minute I had the idea of two ninety-minute episodes to play with, the project not only became more realistic, but also more creatively rewarding. It gave me the time to draw out a situation where the audience could become involved in the intrigue of trying to work out what has happened in Stephen's personal life to make him shut down in the way that he has.'

Eddie clearly felt it had worked. He described to *The Daily Telegraph* how it 'allowed the breadth, over time, for the love story to develop. And that's what I had found astonishing in the novel – the relationship between a young man and a young woman that builds so delicately and intimately and erotically. You cannot rush it. Because if you don't build up its tension, you cannot possibly understand why it has had such a profound impact on this man.'

The effort paid off. '*Birdsong* is remarkable,' wrote Grace Dent in *The Guardian*. 'Unsettling, visceral, a shell-shocked fug of love, loss, then more loss, then the brink of despair, with anything left then battered and blown up again. *Birdsong* switches starkly between two contrasting settings: our hero Stephen Wraysford's youthful trip to drowsy, rural France – all picnics, boating and stolen fumbles with Isabelle, his gnarly host's unappreciated wife (Clémence Poésy) – and first world war trench warfare. Blood, guts, body parts, darkness, morphine, mass graves, the zen-like acceptance of imminent death; elsewhere grown men wailing, clutching photos of sweethearts, bullying, betrayal, biblical hell playing out on Earth.'

Although she didn't think much of the love story, Serena Davies in *The Daily Telegraph* also found it very special. 'The BBC, then, have done something important – they have made an elegiac, lyrical film (that is better than Spielberg's *War Horse*) with which the next generation can associate the war. It aspires to the sentiments of the war poets,' she wrote. '"The poetry is in the pity," as Wilfred Owen had it. And if there is a hint of mawkishness in this, Faulks must first bear responsibility before we lay it at the feet of Auntie.'

There were also some negative vibes, though. As the two main characters were supposed to have had a passionate love affair, there were three sex scenes within the first episode, one of which – as the papers coyly put it – had Poésy 'performing a sex act' on Eddie. The programme had been broadcast after 9 p.m., but nonetheless it caused some ire.

'It is all too easy for them to get hold of it on BBC iPlayer if they want to,' said Vivienne Pattison of Mediawatch-UK. 'All they have to do is tick a box to say they're sixteen and they're away. We are concerned about children's access to TV programmes on the Internet. It's not enough to just put a warning at the start of a programme and make sure it is after the watershed.' It was ironic really – Eddie had played some roles that were much more disturbing than this.

Other critics pointed out that the trenches, while harrowing, could not be compared to the real thing – for a start there weren't any rats in them. But these were minor niggles for what had clearly been a great success.

Anyway, there was no time to rest – the Eddie bandwagon was moving on. To widespread astonishment, it was announced that he was going to play the role of Marius in *Les Misérables* – a musical, which meant that he had to be able to sing. Eddie hastily said that he would be needing 'hardcore lessons' but someone begged to differ: David Bland, the former assistant verger in the College Chapel at Eton, said, 'I can tell you he has got one of the most beautiful voices I have ever heard. He was a chorister in the choir when I was there and has a wonderful voice. While the public may not have heard it yet, they won't be disappointed.' Was there no end to Eddie's talents? Apparently not, as he was about to prove himself in a role very different from anything that had gone before.

CHAPTER ELEVEN

EMPTY CHAIRS AT EMPTY TABLES

Les Misérables was nothing less than a sensation. Based on the 1862 novel of the same name written by the French author Victor Hugo, this has become one of the most successful musicals ever made. The dramatic production of *Les Mis*, as it came to be known, started life as a somewhat obscure French concept album by Alain Boublil and Claude-Michel Schönberg, which had been inspired by the great theatrical impresario Cameron Mackintosh's production of *Oliver!* (based on the Charles Dickens's *Oliver Twist*). This was followed by a short-lived musical stage adaptation directed by the French director Robert Hossein at the Palais des Sports in Paris in 1980, where it garnered audiences totalling half a million people. But it only ran for three months and when it closed down, after the initial booking contract expired, that was pretty much that.

Except that it wasn't. Quite a few people had realised that they were in the presence of something special and so the wheels began to move to mount what would become one of the greatest musicals ever produced. In 1983 Cameron Mackintosh opened *Cats* on Broadway – another contender for one of the truly great musicals of all time – and, flush with success, he received a copy of the original concept album from the Hungarian director Peter Farago, who asked if he would produce an English version. Accounts differ as to what happened next: some have it that Mackintosh immediately recognised the brilliance of what he was hearing, even though he didn't quite understand the words, while others put him down as being more reluctant. At any rate, he eventually conceded there was something in it and agreed that he would produce an English version of the show. So he began to assemble a team, including: Trevor Nunn (now Sir Trevor) – one of the outstanding directors of his generation – and fellow director John Caird, as well as the lyricist James Fenton. Work began but after eighteen months Fenton was replaced by Herbert Kretzmer. At that stage there were only five months before the premiere.

What happened next showed the critics getting it so comprehensively wrong that jokes about their reaction are still made to this day. *Les Misérables* opened on 8 October 1985 in a production by the Royal Shakespeare Company at the Barbican Centre – and the critics hated it. The late Jack

Tinker of the *Daily Mail* called it 'The Glums', a name which has stuck, and although it is meant affectionately now, it certainly wasn't then. Each vied with the others to see who could be ruder: it was 'a lurid Victorian melodrama produced with Victorian lavishness' according to Francis King in *The Sunday Telegraph*, while Michael Ratcliffe in *The Observer* described it as 'a witless and synthetic entertainment'. Others called it 'a load of sentimental old tosh', 'a turgid panorama' and 'a crude cops and robbers epic'.

The public, however, begged to differ. The run sold out; it transferred first to the Palace Theatre and then, in 2004, to the Queen's Theatre. By then the critics realised that maybe they'd been a little too hasty and there might be some merit in the piece after all. *Les Misérables* is now the second longest-running musical in the world after the New York-based and considerably less well-known *The Fantasticks*; it is the longest-running musical in the West End, the second longest-running West End show after *The Mousetrap* and, on 3 October 2010, it celebrated its twenty-fifth anniversary with three concurrent productions in London alone. Needless to say, it has also transferred all over the world.

Considering that level of success, it was absolutely inevitable that one day it would be turned into a film, but it proved to be a complex process. As far back as 1988, Alan Parker's name went forward as a putative director and in 1991 Bruce Beresford was signed up to direct. The following year Cameron said it would be co-produced by Tri-Star Pictures, but all that came to nothing and it was well over a decade before wheels finally began to turn. Finally, in 2005, the project was revived, with Cameron saying that he wanted it to be directed by 'someone who has a vision for the show that will put the show's original team including [him] back to work,' and adding that he wanted the film's audience to make it 'as fresh as the actual show'.

And so the slow process to bring *Les Mis* to the big screen had begun. In 2009 Eric Fellner, one of the producers, started acquiring the film rights, a process that was concluded in 2011. He, Tim Bevan and Debra Hayward then brought the distinguished screenwriter William Nicholson, whose past credits include *First Knight* and *Gladiator*, to work on the script; he produced a first draft within six weeks. The director was Tom Hooper, with whom Eddie had previously worked on *Elizabeth I*, and who had recently had a huge success with *The King's Speech*. Casting began, with some of the biggest names in the business signing up for the production which, right from the start, was clearly going to be one of the major films of the decade.

Les Misérables – as its name implies – is not a comedy. Set it nineteenth-century France, it tells the story of Jean Valjean, aka Prisoner 24601, who is released from prison after serving nineteen years for stealing a loaf of bread and breaks parole after an act of kindness from the Bishop of Digne, swearing that he will turn over a new leaf and lead a good life. In doing so, he incurs the wrath of the prison guard Javert, who swears he will go after him.

Fast forward eight years: Valjean has become a wealthy

factory owner and mayor of the town of Montreuil-sur-Mer but when one of his workers, Fantine, is discovered to be sending money to her illegitimate daughter Cosette, who lives with the untrustworthy Thénardiers and their daughter Éponine, she is dismissed and turns to prostitution. Javert, now a police inspector, arrests her, but Valjean takes pity on her and sends her to hospital, where she is found to be suffering from tuberculosis. Valjean promises to look after Cosette when she dies, which she does shortly afterwards, but also discovers that a man, who is thought to be him, has been arrested. Unable to condemn an innocent man to death, Valjean reveals his true identity but escapes before Javert can arrest him, rescues Cosette and flees to the Bishop of Digne, who gives him and Cosette new identities.

Another nine years on and with Jean Maximilien Lamarque, a government official concerned about the poor, nearing death, two students – Marius Pontmercy and Enjolras – and a street urchin called Gavroche start plotting a revolution. After glimpsing her, Marius falls in love with Cosette, who knows little of her late mother Fantine. He is introduced to her by his friend Éponine, who is in love with Marius. Cosette and Marius profess their love, while Éponine decides to join the revolution. Valjean thinks that Javert has discovered him and flees with Cosette as the revolution begins. Éponine saves Marius's life but sacrifices her own; Javert poses as a rebel and is caught by the real ones and Valjean turns up to save Marius. He is chosen to execute Javert but ends up extending mercy to him and fakes the execution. Government troops move in on the students and kill almost everyone, except Marius, who is saved by Valjean. Javert discovers the two of them but after Valjean refuses to surrender, commits suicide, unable to reconcile his professional duties with his conscience. Valjean reveals his past to Marius, making him promise not to tell Cosette and disappears to save them both; Marius and Cosette marry, discover Valjean's whereabouts and rush to see him. Valjean is dying: he tells Cosette of his past life and is then escorted to paradise by the spirits of Fantine and the Bishop, where he is reunited with the other rebels. The End.

The film had a production budget of $61 million and was shot in various locations around Britain – including Boughton House, Winchester College, Winchester Cathedral Close, Pinewood Studios – and various others, such as Gourdon, Alpes-Maritimes, in France. It goes without saying that there was an enormous amount of excitement surrounding the casting of the new film. Slowly, details began to trickle out: the first big name to emerge was Hugh Jackman, as Valjean, after he auditioned before Cameron in June 2011. Details of the regime he followed to prepare for the role became famous: he lost fifteen pounds and regained thirty to follow his character's development, drank seven litres of water a day, made extensive use of steam rooms and cold baths, and worked with the vocal coach Joan Lader to extend his vocal range from high baritone to tenor.

Next up was Russell Crowe, who was cast as Javert, even though that part had previously seemed destined for

Paul Bettany. Anne Hathaway was Fantine, beating such luminaries as Amy Adams, Jessica Biel, Tammy Blanchard, Kristin Kreuk, Marion Cotillard, Kate Winslet and Rebecca Hall. She was also required to lose twenty-five pounds and had to endure having her hair cut off on camera. Her name had also been linked to Cosette, but she described how 'there was resistance because I was between their ideal ages for the parts – maybe not mature enough for Fantine but past the point where I could believably play Cosette.' In the event, the part of Cosette went to Amanda Seyfried, who remarked, 'In the little time that I had to explain Cosette and give the audience a reason [to see her] a symbol of love and strength and light in this tragedy, I needed to be able to convey things you may not have connected with the show.'

Helena Bonham Carter and Sacha Baron Cohen were cast as the villainous Thénardiers, and Samantha Barks, who had also played the role on stage, was Éponine. 'There was similarities in playing the role [on stage and the screen] – they're the same character – but Éponine in the novel and Éponine in the musical are two kind of different girls, so to me it was the thrill of merging those two together, to get something that still had that heart and soul that we all connect to in the musical, but also the awkward, self-loathing teenager that we see in the novel, trying to merge those two together,' she said. She, too, had to beat a cast of luminaries for the role, which included Scarlett Johansson (who had also been considered for Fantine), Lea Michele, Tamsin Egerton, Taylor Swift and Evan Rachel Wood. Her casting was announced by Cameron, who went on stage during a curtain call for *Oliver!*, then showing at the Palace Theatre in Manchester. It was there that he told Samantha, as well as the delighted audience, that she had just won the role of Éponine.

Eddie was cast as Marius – a role that Aaron Tveit, who played Enjolras, had originally gone for. Anyone who knew anything about his background as a chorister wouldn't have been surprised by the fact that he was cast in a leading role in a musical, but of course publicly he had never done anything similar before, and so eyebrows were raised. Could he actually sing? Well, yes – very well, in fact – but he had not been called upon to do it professionally before.

And Eddie realised that his casting might come as a shock to some and resolved to prove himself in the role. He had had to work hard to get it, too. 'I sang when I was a kid, but I haven't for about ten or twelve years,' he told the *Huffington Post*. 'I saw *Les Mis* when I was nine or ten, however, and wanted to be Gavroche. I loved the piece. I had worked with Tom before in an HBO film about Elizabeth I with Helen Mirren. So I knew Tom and I knew that I would love to play a part. I was on a set in North Carolina and recorded myself on my iPhone, singing this song. It was really just to show my agents, who didn't know I was interested in singing, that I enjoyed singing and wanted to have a go at this part. That was the start of a really rigorous process that I could only describe as *X-Factor* or *American Idol*. The last audition was in front of Tom, Nina Gold, Tim Bevan and Eric Fellner, the producers at Working Title, Cameron Mackintosh, Claude-Michel Schönberg and Alain Boublil. They all sat behind us in a panel. What was extraordinary was that everyone went through that: Hugh, Russell. Samantha Barks, who plays Éponine and has done it so extraordinarily on stage, went through that again.'

The truth was that, with the stakes so high, Eddie wouldn't have got the part if he hadn't proven himself to be totally capable for the role. This was a film based on a stunningly successful musical that had taken decades to get to the screen; an enormous amount of money and professional reputations were at stake and everyone involved knew that they had to get it right. In a way it was reminiscent of the process by which Renée Zellweger landed the title role in *Bridget Jones's Diary* more than a decade previously: there was a great deal of astonishment that a Texan A-lister should have played the part of a hard-drinking, chain-smoking London singleton. At that time, as in the case of *Les Mis*, the producers saw vast numbers of people, as they knew that they had to get the casting spot-on.

Given that Eddie was to perform some show-stopping numbers, they had to make sure that he was up to them, and so his final numbers for the auditions were 'Empty Chairs At Empty Tables' and 'A Heart Full Of Love'. Eddie had rather a wry take on how he got to the high notes. 'Claude-Michel, who composed it, got so passionate and into [the audition] that he made me sing that bit in "One Day More", where I have to come in and grab a flag and sing quite a high note;

a rousing note,' he related. 'I hadn't prepared that. He was like, "Eddie, you must try this!" I thought, "Oh, God." I grabbed my balls and gave it as good a belt as I could.' An interesting technique, but it seemed to pass muster.

'Empty Chairs' was of course a seminal moment in the film, sung alone in the café, after the battle is over and everyone has been killed except Marius and Valjean. Starting with the line, 'There's a grief that can't be spoken,' it is a lament to his dead comrades – to their ideals and to lost dreams – and a reference to his awareness that the terrible conditions in which the poor of Paris lived were to go on. Eddie played a prominent role throughout the film but this solo really was his moment, the point where the spotlight was on him and him alone. It was imperative that he was able to carry it off.

'What was interesting about the shooting of "Les Mis" is that most characters have their seminal song,' Eddie told the *Huffington Post*. 'I listened to the Michael Ball version of "Empty Chairs at Empty Tables" since I was a kid. You'd arrive on set one day and you'd hear the crew going, "Oh my God, have you heard Annie's 'I Dreamed A Dream'? It was *spectacular*!" Gradually, you'd move through the schedule and hear, "Oh, did you hear 'Bring Him Home'? Astounding!" Tom, almost in a sort of sadistic way, kept moving "Empty Chairs" further and further along. I think he was making up for the fact that years ago, when we had worked together before, I had lied to him about my horse-riding prowess. He kept moving it along and then it sits on your shoulder like a gremlin. The day that it came, I knew I had to give it everything. We did about seven takes and Tom said, "I think we got it." I was like, "No, Tom. We have to keep going. I have to literally bleed this song so when I see it in the film and I'm disappointed by it, I know at least I've given everything I can." Tom told me that the last take – the 21st or 23rd take that he used. I quite like that.'

Teasing aside, their working relationship was actually very good and Eddie was only too keen to sing his praises. 'He was incredibly collaborative,' Eddie told the *Huffington Post*. 'Certainly during the rehearsal process, we sat with Tom and the Victor Hugo book adding things. Stuff that didn't work in the musical or plot points from the musical that you don't need to investigate because of the distance from stage to the audience. The fact that, in the book, Marius' grandfather is very wealthy and Marius has given all that up for his political beliefs. Adding those moments with the grandfather in a way to show that this guy had a political agenda that he was willing to give everything up for. Similarly, the moment where he takes the gun powder and threatens to blow up the barricade. That came from the book. Tom was brilliant like that. He's a wonderful leader and team player and everyone brought their elements to it.'

And so to the inevitable question: would he ever do another musical? 'I don't know, man,' Eddie mused. 'It was an extraordinary thing, but it felt like a very specific thing. Never say never, but I'm not sure. I love going to see musicals that could be interpreted, like "Cabaret" [in which he had performed as a student], that aren't the same production.

One of the great things about doing the film version of "Les Mis" was that the more you scrutinise the text and lyrics, it really holds up. So those are the musicals that I enjoy.' Fortunately, the critics were to feel the same.

Les Misérables was by any estimate a stunning success. It earned $148,809,770 in North America and $293,000,000 in other territories, for a worldwide total of $441,809,770. In North America, it opened on 25 December 2012 in 2,808 theatres, breaking the record for the highest opening day gross for a musical film, which had been previously held by *High School Musical 3: Senior Year*. It was also the second highest opening day gross for a film released on Christmas Day and it earned $27.3 million in its opening weekend, placing third behind *Django Unchained* and *The Hobbit: An Unexpected Journey*. Everyone's expectations had been vindicated.

The critics were, on the whole, exceedingly positive: Robbie Collin of *The Daily Telegraph* wrote, '*Les Misérables* is a blockbuster, and the special effects are emotional: explosions of grief; fireballs of romance; million-buck conflagrations of heartbreak. Accordingly, you should see it in its opening week, on a gigantic screen, with a fanatical crowd.' Todd McCarthy of *The Hollywood Reporter* was a little harsher: 'As the enduring success of this property has shown, there are large, emotionally susceptible segments of the population ready to swallow this sort of thing, but that doesn't mean it's good.' Similarly, Manohla Dargis of *The New York Times* was also unconvinced: '[Director Tom]

Hooper can be very good with actors. But his inability to leave any lily ungilded – to direct a scene without tilting or hurtling or throwing the camera around – is bludgeoning and deadly. By the grand finale, when tout le monde is waving the French tricolor in victory, you may instead be raising the white flag in exhausted defeat.'

However, *The Guardian*'s Peter Bradshaw opined, 'Even as a non-believer in this kind of "sung-through" musical, I was battered into submission by this mesmeric and sometimes compelling film.' Kenneth Turan of the *Los Angeles Times* felt it 'is a clutch player that delivers an emotional wallop when it counts. You can walk into the theater as an agnostic, but you may just leave singing with the choir.' Also, Peter Travers of *Rolling Stone* wrote, 'Besides being a feast for the eyes and ears, *Les Misérables* overflows with humor, heartbreak, rousing action and ravishing romance. Damn the imperfections, it's perfectly marvelous.'

Callum Marsh of *Slant* magazine was one of the critics who felt that the singing demands were just too much for some of the stars. 'Flaws – and there are a great many that would have never made the cut were this a perfectible studio recording – are conveniently swept under the rug of candid expression ... the worst quality of *Les Misérables*'s live singing is simply that it puts too much pressure on a handful of performers who frankly cannot sing ... Fisheye lenses and poorly framed close-ups abound in *Les Misérables*, nearly every frame a revelation of one man's bad taste ... One would be hard-pressed to describe this, despite the wealth of beauty on display, as anything but an ugly film, shot and cut ineptly. Everything in the film, songs included, is cranked to 11, the melodrama of it all soaring. So it's odd that this kind of showboating maximalism should be ultimately reduced to a few fisheye'd faces, mugging for their close-up, as the people sing off-key and broken.'

Nevertheless, there was plenty of praise for the singing as well. Anne Hathaway's rendition of 'I Dreamed a Dream' was widely praised. Christopher Orr of *The Atlantic* wrote that 'Hathaway gives it everything she has, beginning in quiet sorrow before building to a woebegone climax: she gasps, she weeps, she coughs. If you are blown away by the scene – as many will be; it will almost certainly earn Hathaway her first Oscar – this may be the film for you.' And Ann Hornaday of *The Washington Post* remarked, 'The centerpiece of a movie composed entirely of centerpieces belongs to Anne Hathaway, who as the tragic heroine Fantine sings another of the memorable numbers.' Claudia Puig of *USA Today* said the actress was 'superb as the tragic Fantine' and Travers described how 'a dynamite Hathaway shatters every heart when she sings how "life has killed the dream I dreamed." Her volcanic performance has Oscar written all over it.' Lou Lumenick of the *New York Post* said it was 'worth seeing for Hathaway alone' and therefore, following all this acclaim, no one was too surprised when she won the Academy Award for Best Supporting Actress. Eddie received his fair share of praise, too, for his singing, which had been until then a talent known only to a few. Bloomberg News felt that

'Eddie Redmayne – most recently seen as the eager young production assistant in *My Week with Marilyn* – delivers by far the most moving and memorable performance in the film as the young firebrand Marius, who, along with his fellow students, is caught up in France's political upheavals in the nineteenth century.'

Others also came in for positive reviews. *Digital Journal* wrote: 'Samantha Barks plays Éponine with such grace, sweetness, and sadness that it is hard to imagine anyone else in the role,' while Claudia Puig of *USA Today* called her 'heartbreakingly soulful'.

When Oscar time came round in 2013, the film did not disappoint. It was nominated for eight Academy Awards – including Best Picture, Best Actor in a Leading Role for Hugh Jackman and Best Original Song – and it went on to win in three categories: Best Supporting Actress for Anne Hathaway, Best Makeup and Hairstyling and Best Sound Mixing. It also won four Baftas, including – again – Anne Hathaway for Best Actress in a Supporting Role. She was unquestionably the real star of the film, albeit one with less screen time than the others, and won numerous awards for her part, including a Golden Globe and a Screen Actors Guild Award. Eddie had also been nominated for a few awards but this wasn't the most important achievement; what mattered most was that he had been given the chance to show that his reach was even wider than had previously been realised, because of his singing talent.

Eddie was on the cusp of real fame, although he didn't

know it yet. As self-deprecating as ever, he told *The Times*, 'Very occasionally someone will stop me and go: "You're an actor, aren't you?" Yup. "What have you been in?" *The Good Shepherd*. "Never heard of it." *Elizabeth: The Golden Age*. "Never heard of it." *Birdsong*. "What's that?" You sit there, reeling off your CV, and they're like: "No, no, no, no." So now, when they say: "You're an actor, aren't you?" I just say, "No."'

He wasn't going to be able to get away with that for much longer, though. Eddie had been part of one of the biggest success stories of the year – and his name was now being put forward for some of the meatiest roles around.

CHAPTER TWELVE

I'M AN ASTRONOMER, NOT AN ASTROLOGER

On 8 January 1942, a child was born who was to become the most famous scientist of his generation: a truly remarkable figure who not only defied the doctors who gave him a two-year life expectancy when he was still in his early twenties, but who also astounded the world by revealing a mind that merely grew in brilliance as his body became ever more debilitated. Stephen William Hawking was born to Frank and Isobel, who were to have two more children, Philippa and Mary, and to adopt another boy, Edward.

During his childhood, Stephen did not initially stand out. Frank became the head of the Division of Parasitology at the National Institute for Medical Research and the family moved to St Albans, where their slightly eccentric lifestyle included travelling around in a converted London taxicab. Hawking did not shine academically at first but soon began to show an aptitude for sciences, eventually winning a scholarship to read physics and chemistry at University College, Oxford – a post he took up at the age of seventeen. For the first time it began to become clear that he was to turn into a man of real brilliance. Initially lonely, he became 'one of the boys' when he began coxing the rowing team and, having neglected his studies, he only just managed to scrape the First he needed to do postgraduate work on cosmology at Cambridge.

Following a trip to Iran, he duly started work at Trinity Hall, Cambridge. It was there that he began to show the symptoms of motor neuron disease (also known as ALS or Lou Gehrig's disease) and, after an initial bout of depression, he determined to battle on and married his first wife Jane Wilde, with whom he went on to have three children. And so began one of the most brilliant scientific careers in the twentieth century, which resulted in numerous awards from all over the world and, of course, works for the layman, including *A Brief History of Time*.

Stephen Hawking's story – that of a brilliant mind trapped in an atrophied body – is famous worldwide. His personal life is also known, including the fact that the marriage ultimately broke down and there was a second marriage to one of his nurses, Elaine Mason, which also ended in divorce. In 1999, Jane, who had lived in Stephen's shadow throughout her life and had had to be carer as much as wife, published a memoir of her own – *Music to Move the Stars: A Life with Stephen* –

which caused a sensation. After Stephen's 2006 divorce from his second wife, he forged a closer relationship with Jane, who had also married again, and an updated version of the book was published under the name of *Travelling to Infinity: My Life with Stephen*.

This was the book on which the film was to be based: an account of how Stephen and Jane got together as students, their marriage and the arrival of children, Jane's growing friendship with Jonathan Hellyer Jones (her second husband) and, ultimately, Stephen's with Elaine. It encompassed all the most notable elements of Stephen's life: the fact that he was originally a cox on the boats, his growing incapacity, the final loss of his voice following a tracheotomy when he had pneumonia, and his growing international fame, first among academic circles – as he postulates that black holes might have been part of the creation of the universe – and then his rise to superstardom following the publication of *A Brief History of Time*.

The film chronicles the divorce but manages to do so in a positive way, leading to some criticism that it was a somewhat sanitised version of events. Some events were indeed changed for dramatic purposes, including details about how they met and the fact that Jane knew about his illness before the relationship began; Eddie's portrayal of Stephen is also said to be somewhat gentler than the real Hawking, who was known to be a very stubborn man (possibly one of the reasons he was able to overcome his problems as much as he did).

Quite clearly, this was a love story, between an extraordinary man and his also pretty extraordinary wife. And the physical transformation that Eddie had to undergo was phenomenal, from the first dropping of a pen – a slight indication that all was not well – to the full-blown illness that was to deprive him of movement and speech.

The film had a long gestation period – over twenty years, in some ways. The screenwriter Anthony McCarten read *A Brief History of Time* in 1988 and developed a fascination with Hawking, which deepened after he read Jane's book. He began working on a screenplay and met with her on numerous occasions. After their mutual agent Craig Bernstein introduced him to the producer Lisa Bruce, the two of them spent a great deal more time with Jane, persuading her to make the film, which they finally managed to do in typically English style: 'It was a lot of conversation, many glasses of sherry and many pots of tea,' said Lisa. Jane finally agreed.

In April 2013, James Marsh came on board as director and immediately saw it for what it was. 'That's really the essence of the story, it's a very unusual love story in a very strange environment, a very strange sort of landscape, and that is I think the abiding theme of the film,' he told *Deadline.com*. 'It is how these two characters, these two real people transcend all the complications and curveballs that life throws at them.'

It was pretty obvious that they were going to need an actor of outstanding ability to carry it off. Eddie's name was in the frame almost immediately and, as he later confessed, he badly wanted the part. He described to *Intelligent Life* how he spent the afternoon in a pub with James: 'It was about four in the afternoon. James said, "What are you having?" I was trying to judge whether to have a proper drink or not. I asked for a beer. He came back with a coffee. I drank about five beers. He drank a lot of coffee. By the time we left, I was drunk and he was wired.' He said he would play the part as if 'everything would be connected to everything. Because it is obviously the most extraordinary challenge and responsibility, to be trusted to tell the story of someone's family, which is also a sensitive and complicated one. And to investigate all these aspects of this iconic human being: the physical, the vocal, the scientific, and then cohere it all in the emotional, because at its heart this is a very unusual love story. Young love, passionate love, family love, love of a subject, but also the failures of love and the boundaries of love.'

Marsh found this amusing but also realised straight away that Eddie would be perfect for the role. 'Very quickly I was persuaded that Eddie was going to do something extraordinary with this role,' he told *Intelligent Life*. 'He's part of a very interesting generation and there were half a dozen actors being discussed for the part ... And the fact that he seemed properly scared. He must have drunk at least four pints in front of me, and that was a nice little indication he was human. There aren't many American actors who would do that.'

Felicity Jones, as Jane, followed shortly afterwards. Emily

Watson and David Thewlis also starred, while Charlie Cox took on the role of Jonathan Hellyer Jones and Maxine Peake was Stephen's second wife, Elaine. The producers were to be Working Title's Tim Bevan, Eric Fellner, Lisa Bruce and Anthony McCarten.

Eddie was delighted to be working with Felicity. 'How I know Felicity is through the Donmar Warehouse,' he told *The Independent*. 'Michael Grandage, who used to run the theatre, he was our great supporter, he gave Felicity and me, both individually, great roles. It was so lovely to have someone who is a friend and whose work I admired, and who I never got to work with, to jump into this with because the stakes felt pretty high.'

It's always a challenge for an actor to play a person who is still living and this role came with a whole set of constraints of its own. Eddie started to do a lot of research into Stephen and ALS, and was his usual self-deprecatory self about it too. 'I'd been at Cambridge so I'd seen Stephen at a distance and knew that he studied black holes, but I'd been studying Renaissance paintings,' he told *Wired*. 'I realized I was ignorant enough not to realize it was ALS, not to realize that he'd once been entirely healthy, not to realize this extraordinary story behind this icon,' Redmayne says. 'I found it deeply riveting. It's not glossed, I actually found it quite real ... I felt like it was a scrutiny of love in all of its guises.'

Filming began in October 2013 in and around the beautiful city of Cambridge, with the ancient and imposing university playing the backdrop to the story of one of its most famous sons. New Court featured, as did The Backs along the river, St John's College and other locations that would have been familiar to Eddie from his own time as a student there. Everyone was pleased with how it was going but it was not until filming was well underway that Eddie finally met Stephen and his own account of it proves, if proof were needed, that his new status had certainly not gone to his head. In fact, he came across – in his own words – as a combination of gauche and starstruck, and very endearing with it, too.

'I was terrified, because I'd made choices, in terms of his physical decline and his character, that I couldn't now go back on,' he told *Intelligent Life*. 'So I was thinking "oh God, what if I meet him and it changes everything, is this going to undermine all the work I've done?" Then his carers, who are lovely, took me in to meet him, and the first thing I do is over-apologise for the fact that someone who'd studied art history is playing this great scientific mind ... And then, for some reason, I hear myself informing him he was born on January 8th, because I've been talking about science and religion in our film and he makes this point in his book "My Brief History" about how he was born 300 years to the day after Galileo, and then I tell him I was born on January 6th, I don't know why I say it, but I do, "so we're both Capricorns", and then the second it comes out of my mouth I'm like, "Fuck. What did I just say to Stephen Hawking?" And there is this punishing four or five minutes as he blinks away. Finally, the voice says, with killer timing: "I am an astronomer, not an astrologer." And it's just, the idea that he might think the guy playing him in a biopic thinks he's Mystic Meg ... I don't think I ever will get over it.' He needn't have worried. In actual fact Stephen enjoyed the film so much (and in so doing paid tribute to Eddie's powerful performance) that he allowed the film-makers to use his actual synthesised voice, which is heard in the film.

But this also brought home to Eddie that although Stephen was disabled, there was nothing of the victim about him. 'He's in complete control,' Eddie recalled. 'Not only is he clearly adored by all the people around him, it's amazing to see how flirtatious he is, but also he emanated wit and humour and this sort of energy. Even though he can use very few muscles now, it's one of the most expressive faces I've ever seen. He's very funny. With his voice machine, there's no intonation, no way of delivering something with nuance, so all he has is the capacity to press play. Watching how he navigates that is amazing; his timing is magnificent. He is the king of the one-liner. He's cool. He's fucking cool.'

He was also helpful, giving Eddie advice on how to play him, which led to a vigorous debate with the makers of the film about how far the actor would be able to go in the reality of the portrayal. 'He told me that his voice had been very slurry, but we hadn't taken that on board so much,' Eddie told *The Independent*. 'We'd watched some of the documentary material where his voice was almost incomprehensible. So I could go back to the producers, and more importantly director James Marsh, and say we need to take this on board, but we still didn't go quite so far because they didn't want to use subtitles, but it did give me permission to really go and be pretty strong with that, because it was important for Stephen [Hawking] and screenwriter Anthony McCarten that we show the illness in full ... Although he can move only a few muscles, he sort of emanates this vitality and humour, this wit and flirtatiousness.'

The Stephen seen at the beginning of the film is a far cry from the Stephen Hawking that people are familiar with today. But the young Stephen was a bit of a fop in some ways and certainly conscious of his appearance – something else that was news to Eddie. 'I was surprised to learn that when Stephen was a young man, he was fashionably dressed, and an icon of cool,' he told the *Daily Mail*. 'There are some photographs of him and Jane in a punt in Cambridge when they were younger, and they looked amazing. He used to wear a blue velvet jacket, which we copied for the film, which with those glasses looked fabulous. His dress sense never left him – I wore seventy-seven different outfits throughout the film. I learned that when he was twenty-one, Stephen decided to grow his nails as an act of defiance. So I grew mine, too, and kept them over-long throughout filming, although there is only one shot in the finished film where you see them.'

Eddie, rightly, received a huge amount of praise for the portrayal of Stephen's physical deterioration: from the healthy days of whizzing on a bicycle around Cambridge to being hunched in a wheelchair, unable to speak without the aid of a computerised voice box. Unsurprisingly, he had some help with all of this. He spent hours looking at videos of Stephen, especially when he was suspended in zero gravity, and worked with a specialist, who explained how the cosmologist's body was slowly withering away, as well as with Alex Reynolds, who had choreographed the zombies in *World War Z*. To make matters more complicated, filming was not done chronologically, so Eddie had to know what condition Stephen was in at any point in his life: 'So on the first day of filming in the morning you're healthy, by lunchtime you're on two sticks and then in the afternoon you're in the chair.'

And all the while the responsibility to the real Stephen was there. The point about the story was actually not Stephen's disability but his achievements and the former could not be allowed to overshadow the latter. Alex helped him so that he could 'try to map out Stephen's specific physical decline, fix it in the details and embed all of that, so that I can forget it, because the illness is the least important part of life, as far as he's concerned,' Eddie told *Intelligent Life*. 'Fifty years ago he was given two or three years to live, and he's always chosen to look forward despite the guillotine over his head. It's important to have all the physical stuff down so that Felicity [Jones, as Jane] and I are free to play the human story.'

In fact, Eddie could not speak highly enough of his illustrious subject. 'Above and beyond anything, what you take away from the experience is – and this is the first time

I've talked about it, really – that tension,' he told *Wired*. 'It makes the room ripe. It's like everyone is slightly on their toes. You're paying attention. You've always got an eye on what he's observing and "Is he going to say something?" But then there's what he emanates, which is humour, acerbic wit, killer timing, and a love of life. When Felicity came in he was just like, "Hi. I'm a rockstar," basically. And I very promptly got shoved aside.'

Reading between the lines, Stephen really seemed to be impressed by Eddie's commitment to the role, as he clearly took it very seriously. He started by watching footage of Hawking and reading *A Brief History of Time*. He visited a neurology clinic – the Queen Square Centre for Neuromuscular Diseases in London – where he talked to MND patients, and put himself through some real discomfort in his preparation for the role. 'We also worked with an amazing make-up designer, Jan Sewell, who explained that because Stephen moves one side of his face a lot more than the other, that side would be more lined and it also became more muscular,' he told the *Daily Mail*. 'It was pretty painful, twisting my body in the wheelchair the way Stephen does, but I had an osteopath to help me through it.

'But however uncomfortable it was, at the end of the day I was able to stand up, get out of the wheelchair and relax in a hot bath, which most people who are suffering from this don't, and that was something I never forgot.

'In spite of the personal difficulties he has to face, the overriding thing when I met Stephen was this extraordinary, razor-sharp wit and formidable humour. There is a kind of mischief, a Lord of Misrule quality that I tried to bring into my performance after spending time with him. We even adapted the script after that first meeting to make him funnier.'

Eddie commented on the work he did with an osteopath, Dan Studdard, by saying, 'I had to train my body like a dancer but learn to shorten muscles instead of stretch them,' he told *The Observer*. The decision was taken that although his character didn't know it, Stephen would actually be suffering from the disease from before the film began and so the viewer, knowing what is going to happen, will notice the odd clumsy moment on screen that Stephen the character does not yet understand. 'The problem with motor neurone disease is they don't know when it starts,' Eddie told *The Observer*. 'People go into hospital having fallen but get wrapped up and sent away, unless they're seen by an incredibly astute doctor. It is only when several things begin to go wrong that it'll be diagnosed.'

From very early on, it was obvious to everyone involved that they were creating something special. The feedback from early screenings was that Eddie's portrayal of Stephen was almost uncanny; Stephen himself said that at times he could hardly tell himself and Eddie apart. His ex-wife Jane, who had written the book on which the film was based, was wry: 'They made a beautiful film and I had to reconcile myself to the compromises that one has to make for the film industry,' she told *The Guardian*. 'Stephen's colleagues all became one character called Brian who is always there as his companion. Sadly, I didn't seem to have any friends or relations at all.' But she liked Felicity's portrayal of her as much as Stephen liked Eddie's: 'When they were filming, she [Felicity Jones, who played Jane] came to dinner several times and we talked and we talked. I thought, "What is she going to make of me?" But she is a method actress and when I saw her on screen in those first shots when she arrives at the party I was just astounded. I thought, "She's stolen my personality!" because she had my mannerisms, she had my speech patterns. It was a very weird experience.'

Felicity, too, found it a profoundly moving experience. 'I remember saying to Eddie a couple of months after shooting had ended: I am still thinking about Jane! It takes a bit of time to rediscover who you are afterwards,' she told *Esquire*. 'Jane has a certain energy and eccentricity I wanted to capture. She has this incredibly idiosyncratic way of moving and talking. I wanted her to feel almost like a ballerina, like she was dancing through the first act [when her and Hawking meet as students]. But I also loved playing her later, after twenty-five years caring for Stephen, when her sense of humour has become more caustic after all the prejudice they experience.'

And as the film became a major topic of conversation in the movie world – and was tipped for an Oscar – she was well-nigh ecstatic. 'I love this film so much,' she said. 'James [Marsh, the director] made us such a part of the process. It felt very collaborative and I feel very invested in it on many levels. I'm just excited people care about it. You can't really define moments in your own life, can you? You just experience things as they happen,' she continued. 'It's lovely to have made something people have a visceral response to. It's just very exciting. You don't get to make films that are purely character-driven, it's very rare, and so I am revelling in it, actually.'

Meanwhile, both leading actors remained acutely conscious that they had a responsibility to the people they were portraying. 'There were so many levels of anxiety,' Eddie told *The Daily Telegraph*. 'You're playing someone that people know, he's also an icon, he's also living, he's a scientist of extraordinary talent. And Felicity and I felt across the board a responsibility to everyone. Jane and Jonathan [Jones, her second husband] had us for dinner, a wonderful moment at which I arrived at their home and found Felicity in Jane's wardrobe, Jane having brought down her wedding dress. And when people are that kind to you, it ramps up the sense of your not wanting to let them down.'

The Theory of Everything actually premiered at the Toronto International Film Festival on 7 September 2014 before a limited release in the all-important North American market in November. It was released in just five theatres and earned a very respectable $207,000. 'We are very, very pleased,' said Jim Orr, head of distribution at Focus Features, which had acquired distribution rights in the US. 'It's resonating with audiences and the [exit] surveys we conducted showed that [the film] played very well across all demographics. It has outstanding performances with great direction by James

Marsh. I believe the performances, the film itself and the director will be getting Academy attention.' That was a canny view: from then on, the only way was up. A much bigger release came at the end of November, and from then on, the talk was all about Oscars.

It was clear that a major event was taking place. *Intelligent Life* asked: would he be able to handle his new status? 'I feel very lucky,' he said, slightly non-committally. 'Nothing has happened overnight, it's the smallest of shifts. I've just put one foot in front of the other over the past decade and managed to keep working, and working with great people. So yeah, gradually, there's being photographed surreptitiously on the Tube and it ending up online. But that's a very small price to get to do what you're passionate about.' Anyway, there was no turning back now.

The critics could not praise the film highly enough. Leslie Felperin of *The Hollywood Reporter* felt it was, 'A solid, duly moving account of their complicated relationship, spanning roughly twenty-five years, and made with impeccable professional polish.' *The Daily Telegraph*'s Tim Robey loved it, saying, 'In its potted appraisal of Hawking's cosmology, *The Theory of Everything* bends over backwards to speak to the layman, and relies on plenty of second-hand inspiration. But it borrows from the right sources, this Theory. And that's something.' *Deadline.com*'s Pete Hammond wrote: 'To say the response here [in Toronto] was rapturous would not be understating the enthusiasm I heard – not just from pundits but also Academy voters with whom I spoke. One told me he came in with high expectations for a quality movie and this one exceeded them.'

Catherine Shoard of *The Guardian* remarked, 'Redmayne towers: this is an astonishing, genuinely visceral performance which bears comparison with Daniel Day-Lewis in *My Left Foot*.' And Lou Lumenick, of the *New York Post*, described it as 'tremendously moving and inspirational'. Justin Chang of *Variety* opined, 'A stirring and bittersweet love story, inflected with tasteful good humour.'

There were some naysayers who thought the focus was too much on relationships and not enough on theoretical physics. Alonso Duralde of *The Wrap* said, 'Hawking's innovations and refusal to subscribe to outdated modes of thinking merely underscore the utter conventionality of his film biography.' Eric Kohn of *Indiewire* felt that 'James Marsh's biopic salutes the famous physicist's commitment, but falls short of exploring his brilliant ideas.' Dennis Overbye of *The New York Times* opined, 'The movie doesn't deserve any prizes for its drive-by muddling of Dr Hawking's scientific work, leaving viewers in the dark about exactly why he is so famous. Instead of showing how he undermined traditional notions of space and time, it panders to religious sensibilities about what his work does or does not say about the existence of God, which in fact is very little.' But of course, the point of the film was to show the man behind the scientist: Stephen Hawking is not just a cold-blooded genius who understands things the rest of us wouldn't have a clue about, but a flesh-and-blood man who was married twice, and had children and a personal life, as well as a professional one.

Eddie continued to praise Stephen, constantly saying how impressed he had been with him while at the same time laughing at himself for his previous ignorance. 'He has the sharpest mind I've ever encountered,' he told *The Big Issue*. 'You can see the complication between how quick his response is and then the time delay having to spell out that response using just his eye muscle. In the few hours we spent together he said maybe eight or nine sentences. It was me filling the silence that was catastrophic.'

With regard to public misperception as to who Stephen really was, he commented, 'I was in the same position myself. I recognised his voice and his icon-status from *The Simpsons* and that he had done things with black holes but that was the limit of my knowledge. I knew the only way to get close to authentically representing the person we think we know was to uncover the parts that we didn't. I think the discoveries he has made have been utterly, utterly astounding, but the fact he's managed to translate these things to laymen like myself, people who are really useless at science and gave it up as a kid. The idea of democratising science is massive for him and that combined with his extraordinary capacity to overcome these brutal physical obstacles is certainly for me where his fame comes from.'

And so to the great man himself: Professor Stephen Hawking. In an interview with the *Huffington Post*, he gave his views on the film and it turned out everyone came out pretty well. 'I was rather surprised that a major film company should want to make a film about me,' he said. 'At first, I was worried because it was based on a book by my ex-wife, Jane, but I was reassured when I read the script, and even more when I saw a first cut of the film. It was surprisingly honest about our marriage, and my fight with ALS, or motor neurone disease. I thought Eddie Redmayne portrayed me very well. He spent time with ALS sufferers so he could be authentic. At times, I thought he was me. Felicity made a very charming Jane.

'To my surprise, I was very impressed by the film and by Eddie's commitment. It's a human interest story, success against the odds. It shows that disability can be no handicap. I liked the script. It reflects our struggle to bring up three children in normality, despite my disability. But that placed a great strain on our marriage.' Stephen was probably the most important critic of all, to Eddie at least, but it was clear – he had got the approval he needed the most.

One slightly unexpected outcome of it all was that Eddie started to be perceived as an expert on Hawking, not least on the story of his remarkable survival. He was always careful to make it clear, as gently as he could, that this was not the case. Once as he was asked how it could be possible that Stephen is still alive, over fifty years after he was given two years to live, he replied, 'People don't know whether it is to do with the specific strain of the illness. There is another narrative that says it is to do with his drive. But remember, he has extraordinary nursing care and direct contact with

Addenbrooke's Hospital in Cambridge.' In other words – he didn't know and he didn't want to speculate.

And so to award season, where the film pretty much cleaned up. At the 87th Academy Awards it was nominated for Best Picture, Best Actor for Eddie Redmayne (which he won), Best Actress for Jones, Best Adapted Screenplay for McCarten and Best Original Score for Jóhann Jóhannsson. The film was also nominated for ten British Academy Film Awards, five Critics' Choice Movie Awards and three Screen Actors Guild Awards. At the 72nd Golden Globe Awards, Redmayne won Best Actor – Motion Picture Drama and Jóhannsson won Best Original Score. The film and Felicity received nominations, too.

This was the film that catapulted Eddie into the mega-league, the A-list. He became part of the very small category of actors whose name is enough to get a film funding and to carry it on their own. His fame, which had been increasing steadily, now shot out, as he cultivated new fans and amazed more and more people, who recognised one of the truly great film performances in decades. Projects were lining up. And Eddie's love life was looking pretty good, too.

CHAPTER THIRTEEN

EDDIE
IN LOVE

As he turned thirty, while still looking on the young side for his age, Eddie was becoming a very handsome man. He had always been aesthetically pleasing – he hadn't been chosen as a Burberry model for nothing – but like so many men past the first flush of extreme youth, he was filling out in all the right places and generally coming into his own. His name had continued to be linked with various women, but he remained coy about his love life, just as he was always dismissive about his general level of attractiveness. Asked how it felt to be a sex symbol he told *The Times*, 'Um. Very flattering. If it's true ... OK. Right ... I have lots of friends. Who are actors. And I have a sense of their profile. Andrew [Garfield, of *The Amazing Spider-Man* fame]. Tom [Sturridge, fiancé of Sienna Miller]. With them, you see it as a viewer. When you're in it, you genuinely don't see it. There are lovely people who turn up at events I do. Girls. And that's flattering … It's incredibly flattering. Oh, come on.'

And had he always been the centre of female attention? 'Absolutely not. No, no, no. And I'm still not. But I hate that thing where actors say, "Oh, I was so ugly and disgusting. Oh, I was bullied as a child and I was totally revolting." You're like, "No, you're f***ing not. You're the face of some make-up brand." I feel like I was mid-ranking. I would place myself mid-rank.' A growing number of people were beginning to think that was unduly modest.

By January 2012, Eddie had been single for some years, despite being linked to a host of women including Carey Mulligan, Taylor Swift (which he point-blank denied) and the model Cara Delevingne, with whom he cavorted in some Burberry advertisements. 'Christopher [Bailey] wanted something playful from the shoot and so Cara and I had a genius couple of days fooling around. Hopefully the enjoyment we had is reflected in the campaign,' said Eddie brightly, but it was never entirely clear if the fooling around was just for the camera or went on behind the scenes as well. At any rate, if something had happened, it certainly wasn't serious.

However, Eddie was a serious person at heart: he might have been appreciative of the female form but he never developed a reputation as a lothario. He was ready for a new romance and the person with whom he was to have that romance was right under his nose. While he was still at

Eton, he had met the pretty Hannah Bagshawe, who was at a local school nearby; they went their separate ways, however, when Eddie went off to Cambridge and Hannah went to the University of Edinburgh to read English Literature and French. Nevertheless, they had stayed in touch and finally, around the beginning of 2012 – just as Eddie's star was really beginning to rocket upwards and Hannah was working as a publicist – they became a couple. They were acknowledged as such when they appeared together in public for the first time at the *Les Mis* premiere. He was growing up in other ways, too, having bought his first flat. Clearly, domesticity was beginning to appeal.

Some years later Eddie gave an interview in which he revealed that their relationship began around the time he was working on *Les Mis*. 'I'd finished rehearsals and was about to start shooting in a few days and so I said to myself, "I'm going to go to Florence for a quick break and write or do something like that,"' he told the *Daily Mail*. 'Before I went, Hannah and I were on a sort of date – we'd been good friends for twelve years – and we had a wonderful evening and I suddenly said, "You don't want to come to Florence with me next week, do you?" She said, "That's absurd, you don't mean it." I said, "Yes I do!" So our first proper date was in Florence. That was three years ago and we couldn't be happier.'

Hannah was, in fact, quite the high-flyer, which was fortunate given that she was about to step out into the public eye – no place for the faint-hearted. As it turned out, though, she'd already spent some years advising others on just that. According to *Businessweek*, 'Ms. Hannah Bagshawe served as Global Head of Public Relations of Mergermarket Ltd. Ms. Bagshawe served as Head of Communications Europe for Mergermarket Ltd. Ms. Bagshawe was responsible for all Communications/PR in Europe, the Middle East & Africa, across Mergermarket Group. She served for several investment banks including Goldman Sachs, Credit Suisse and Societe Generale before joining Mergermarket in August 2006.' Like George Clooney, who at around the same time was announcing his engagement to the human rights lawyer Amal Alamuddin, he was marrying a woman of substance. More latterly, Hannah has worked as an antiques dealer.

Even so, the couple kept their relationship relatively out of the limelight – a sensible move as many a celebrity relationship has withered and died under the scrutiny of the spotlight. Therefore, it was behind the scenes that their bond deepened, until it became clear to both of them that each had found 'The One'. By May 2014 both were ready to take the next step and, as befits someone coming from as traditional a background as Eddie's, the news appeared in the most old-fashioned way, via an announcement in *The Times*: 'Mr E.J.D. Redmayne and Miss H.J. Bagshawe. The engagement is announced between Edward, son of Mr and Mrs Richard Redmayne of London, and Hannah, daughter of Mr Nicholas Bagshawe and Mrs Caryl Bagshawe, both of London.' It was reported that Eddie had done everything else the traditional way as well, asking permission from Hannah's father before the proposal and, rather romantically, going down on bended knee. Hannah's engagement ring was revealed to the public for the first time when the couple attended Wimbledon: it was a large square diamond, both opulent and tasteful at the same time – much like the couple themselves, in fact.

News of the engagement came as no surprise to those in the know. 'He had been planning on it for a while,' a source told *US Weekly*. 'They have a very relaxed and supportive relationship ... they seemed to have always known they were going to spend the rest of their lives together.' Meanwhile, when Eddie was asked if it was a good idea to marry someone who was not a thespian, he replied, 'I don't think who one marries is a decision. It is how you feel.' That is indeed true, but that said, the fact that Hannah was not an actress might well have been a good thing. Acting is a notoriously unstable profession and to have two members of the family worrying about where the next piece of work would be coming from might have been a little bit too much. Anyway, he was clearly utterly smitten. 'I'm desperate,' he told *E! News*. 'I'm jumping at the bit. I can't wait to be married.'

The pair continued to keep it low-key, but the news did get out that they married at the private club Babington House near Bath, in Somerset, in December 2014. It is a glamorous venue, much loved by the celebrity crowd, a number of whom – Professor Green, Zoe Ball and James Cordon, to name but a few – have got married there. The snow-clad winter scene was enchanting: a 'winter wonderland' complete with snow and decorated with lit candles, created by a special-effects team. The service was conducted at 5.30 p.m. in front of a small group of family and close friends but, in a rare moment of showbiz consciousness, various minders were present to protect Hannah's dress from being seen by the public. This was, however, due to a desire for privacy rather than because of any celebrity magazine deal, the mere mention of which evoked a horrified reaction from Eddie. As for the time of year, 'We like the hymn *In The Bleak Midwinter* and wanted an excuse to sing that at a wedding,' Eddie explained. He was pictured outside the event, looking typically dapper in morning dress and lilac tie.

Hannah, as the bride is traditionally allowed to be, was late, although according to Eddie, that was nothing unusual: 'My wife has never been on time for anything in her life,' he told Ellen DeGeneres. 'She was a good half-hour late. Her grandfather had to be held back from going and summoning her. Everyone else was really stressed, but I was kind of relaxed knowing that she'd never been on time for pretty much anything in her life.'

The pair were the absolute antithesis of the Hollywood couple who can't leave the house without alerting a publicist; life continued in its low-key way but, given that *The Theory of Everything* was now out, Eddie was beginning to attract a huge amount of notice. Even so, they managed to slip away for a brief winter honeymoon: 'We went skiing over Christmas,' he told Ellen DeGeneres. 'We went to the Alps, which was such a beautiful idea, but unfortunately there was no snow. But that was just an excuse to take long lunches, drink a lot of red wine, and have a lot of fondue.' They couldn't stay away too long, though – they had to rush back to London to attend the Golden Globes.

Undeniably, domesticity did suit him. Although – apart from the odd moment spent agonising over his roles – Eddie had never been a particularly angst-ridden type, now he was visibly more relaxed. Whatever happened on set, he had someone to go home to and, he admitted, Hannah was helping him to keep his feet on the ground. 'There was a moment yesterday where I was in rehearsal and my wife was calling me because our dishwasher broke down … So in the process of trying to focus on my craft, I was dealing with the blocked pipes,' Eddie told *E! News*.

It was the ideal antidote to the fuss that has turned many an actor's head and she was also fretting over her new husband, who had had to become very thin to play Hawking, telling him he had to eat. 'I said: "Baby, I've got loads of sushi and juices." And she was like: "That's not what I'm talking about! I'm talking about a f***ing gigantic bowl of spaghetti bolognese and a burger",' Eddie recalled.

Hannah's presence was an excellent thing because his head could certainly have been turned by everything else that was going on around him. Eddie had been in one of the two big science movies that year; the other was *The Imitation Game* – about the great scientist Alan Turing, who broke the enigma code in World War II – starring his friend and (friendly) rival Benedict Cumberbatch. As such, the two of them were asked to present prizes for achievements in science.

'Ben and I went and presented at the Breakthrough Prizes, these huge science awards,' Eddie told *The Daily Telegraph*. 'Ben was presenting a $3 million mathematics prize and I was presenting a $3 million physics prize, and both of us looked at each other and said, "What are we doing here?" I was sitting on the table next to this gigantic investor, who was chatting to a gentleman who'd single-handedly made a major breakthrough in curing cancer. I was like, "I'm an actor? You just keep talking."' But it didn't matter that he wasn't a great scientist – the glare of his celebrity was now so strong that everyone wanted a piece of him.

Hannah, too, gave every indication of coping with her new position with aplomb. By virtue of being married to Eddie, she began being judged on her appearance – just as actresses are – except, of course, that she was not an actress. It is an unnerving experience, even for the most accomplished red-carpet star, but when you're not used to it, it can be an ordeal – and the duo were appearing on quite a few red carpets at that stage. Still, somehow, Hannah, who is blessed with naturally good looks, managed to take it all in her stride.

Eddie, who had gained a reputation as quite the snappy dresser himself, was very aware of the pressures on his new wife. But according to him, she was more than capable of dealing with them. 'She is so mellow with this stuff,' he said as the two arrived in Los Angeles ahead of the Oscars in February 2015. 'I think I get more, like, sort of nervous about it than she does. She is so beautiful and looks amazing in whatever she wears as far as I'm concerned so she's kind of chilled out about it. She's like relatively calm but I think she is very excited about the prospect of wearing quite a beautiful dress.' In the event, of course, she did exactly that.

In fact, Hannah's interest in clothes was to help Eddie, as well. He had always dressed well and had been rather delighted when his stint modelling with Burberry had resulted in him getting free clothes. He also featured on Best Dressed lists, ranking 33rd in *Vanity Fair*'s 2014 list and shooting up to number one in *GQ*'s 2015 version. When he gave interviews, journalists quite frequently commented on how well-turned-out he was. But, of course, he was colour-blind, and therefore he occasionally needed a little bit of help. Hannah was only too happy to oblige. 'I'm confused with colours,' he said in an interview before the pair got married. 'When I go out to premieres and events, I have to check with my girlfriend that the trousers match the top … I recently wore a blue suit – and I had to ask her if it was really blue rather than purple. She assured me it was blue. I could not tell the difference. I'm lucky to be with someone who is very supportive.'

And his sense of style was getting him noticed elsewhere: in 2015 Eddie joined the ranks of Nicole Kidman and George Clooney in becoming an ambassador for the exclusive watch brand Omega. It was an appropriate match: 'I'm always on time,' he told Italian *Grazia*. 'On the contrary, I'm always afraid to be late. The night I won the Oscar, I left the hotel so early that there was no one there: I waited for two hours wandering around Beverly Hills. My dream is a scheduled life. My wife teases me, because working in the cinema means, on the contrary, being flexible. On the set I wake up at 5 a.m. and I have a monastic lifestyle. But if I had more time for me, I'd address it to painting and playing the piano, that I love very much.'

The same interviewer asked him what he was like as a husband and it sounded as if Hannah had lucked out: 'Very romantic,' he said. 'And a beginner: we've been married for only six months. But Hannah has been my rock for a long time. When I'm not working, I like to cook for her. I'm not good, but it's great for her to find everything ready when she comes home. When I'm filming, on the contrary, I'm a rather useless husband.'

Eddie and Hannah married around the time *The Theory of Everything* came out and just before the hysteria over the awards season began: he needed someone in the background to keep him sane. The world was beginning to change in the way it reacted to him and he was becoming increasingly aware of this. For example, when he got off a flight in 2015, he recounted, 'I fell asleep, and when I woke up the man next to me asked, "Excuse me, are you someone important?" I must have looked confused. He explained: "I'm asking because the stewardesses came over and were watching you sleep."'

This changing status came as almost everything happened to Eddie all at once. First marriage and then a slew of awards, culminating in the Oscar – it was hardly surprising when Eddie said, in the course of one of the numerous awards bashes he was attending in Beverly Hills, 'I'm so ecstatic right now. I've had the best few months of my life.'

Is there yet more happiness to come? At the time of writing Hannah was rumoured to be pregnant, mainly on the basis that she appeared to be sporting a tiny bump and she was seen making several toasts with water rather than wine. Eddie's publicist refused to confirm or deny but, whatever the case, the couple, deeply traditional and very happy with each other, are almost certainly going to be looking at starting a family.

But for Eddie there was no time to waste: even before the furore had subsided in the wake of his Oscar win, he was pictured hard at work on set. He was now able to take on projects that a lesser-known actor probably wouldn't have managed to land, such as a documentary about art. People were queuing up to work with him and he was also wooed by the people in charge of the world's favourite wizarding series ... Eddie was in his element. He was the golden boy, indisputably at the top of his game – and deserving of it, come to that.

CHAPTER FOURTEEN

POTTERING ABOUT

It's always a bad sign when a film's release is delayed, and so it was not surprising when *Jupiter Ascending* – a sci-fi film in which Eddie played Balem Abrasax, Emperor of the House of Abrasax – was put back twice and it turned out to be a stinker. This was a film that also starred Sean Bean, with whom of course Eddie had worked before, as Stinger Apini: 'half human and half honeybee' – and the fact that one of the characters is a bee should perhaps have signalled to someone that it was time for a rethink. In fairness, the film had some big names attached to it; directed by Andy and Lana Wachowski, and also starring Channing Tatum and Mila Kunis, it was no one's finest hour. It had actually been made before *The Theory of Everything* but best and kindest, perhaps, to draw a veil over it and move on. Everyone else certainly did.

And anyway, Eddie was becoming involved in a series of very worthwhile projects, especially since his growing fame was giving him a chance to branch out – or rather, reach back to one of his first loves: art. The documentary-maker Margy Kinmonth had seen him in the play *Red*, as well as *Birdsong* and *Les Mis*, and thought he would be ideal to present a series in war art. She had form when it came to tracking down notable presenters, having bagged Sir Ian McKellen and Prince Charles in the past, and now she was on to Eddie. She had him in mind for something about Rothko or war art for the *Perspectives* series on ITV. 'Two years ago I went to see Eddie's agent,' she told the *Radio Times* on the eve of broadcast. 'But then a long time went past because Eddie was shooting the Hawking film. It was hard to get him so I wrote him a letter and it went back and forth a bit but he agreed to meet me.' This, incidentally, was another indication of his changed status: there was to be no more banging on doors on Eddie's part. Now people were clamouring to meet him.

In the event, the two agreed to focus on Paul Nash, which Eddie was keen on as he had covered that period in his degree. He had also revisited the battlefields of north-west France during the preparation for *Birdsong*, solemnly reflecting on the fact that had he been born a century earlier, he might have met his end there too. 'It was extraordinary wandering around where so many people were killed,' he told the *Radio Times*. 'You can't help but find a weird beauty in it and I think that must have been one of the dilemmas. It's something that Nash talks about, it's something that Nevinson talks about –

how in this incomprehensible and, as they say, indescribable context, you could find beauty. It [the frontline war] was unspeakable, hopeless, godless. I'm not sure it's possible to understand the true experience of being a war artist, but I do know that we lost so much formidable talent; so many young men who never got to see their potential fulfilled.'

The programme won a great deal of kudos, featuring as it did the artists Paul Nash, Stanley Spencer, John Singer Sargent, Henry Tonks, CRW Nevinson and David Bomberg, as well as contemporary artists. These included George Butler, who worked in Syria, Graeme Lothian, who worked in Afghanistan, reportage artist Julia Midgley and the official war artist Peter Howson, who worked in Bosnia and whose work was censored. It garnered good reviews, too: 'In the affecting – if not exactly scholarly – programme, Redmayne, a Cambridge history of art graduate, looked at pieces from the past two centuries,' wrote Sally Newall in *The Independent on Sunday*. 'His main focus was the First World War, a period he portrayed in an adaptation of Sebastian Faulks's novel *Birdsong* in 2012. He told us that preparing for the role he found art the most effective tool to immerse himself in the era: "To convey intimately what is often beyond description."'

Marina Vaizey, of *theartsdesk.com*, was impressed. 'Narrating this documentary chiefly concerned with the art of the First World War, Oscar-winning actor Eddie Redmayne told us that the art described the indescribable, conveying what is beyond description,' she wrote. 'If that sounds unbearably fey it isn't at all, for the surprise and interest of this programme was in fact two-fold: Redmayne himself and some quite unexpected facts. Redmayne revealed that he read art history as a Cambridge undergraduate, had an early ambition to be a museum curator, and was further inspired to take a hard look at the period under review by his role in the BBC's dramatisation of Sebastian Faulks's Great War novel, *Birdsong*.'

And *The Times* wrote in a preview of the programme, 'Here, Redmayne – articulate, informed and animated – looks at paintings by those men, as well as others, including the modernist David Bomberg, whose art responded to "the weaponry of the new machine world". There is an evocative scene where he travels to Flanders and visits Sanctuary Wood, scene of one of the war's bloodiest battles, in darkness, with Nash's *We Are Making a New World* superimposed over the wood so it looks as if Redmayne is walking through Nash's painting.'

There were many more positive reviews, with quite a few expressing surprise that Eddie was not just a pretty face but an educated man who actually knew what he was talking about. Until then only a handful of people had known his background as a history-of-art student at Cambridge, but in the wake of the success of *The Theory of Everything*, interest in him had exploded – and better still, the more the public found out about him, the more the public seemed to like him. There was nothing assumed about his manner of easy-going frankness combined with acres of charm; what you saw was what you got: Eddie was a nice man, educated and cultural, and he really did know a lot about art.

But of course, the day job remained the priority and it was not long after the Oscar ceremony that Eddie was to perform as a woman again, this time in the lead role in *The Danish Girl*, based on David Ebershoff's 2000 novel of the same name and due to be released in November 2015. It was right back up there with some of Eddie's more unconventional choices: it was based on the true story of the artist Einar Wegener in 1920s Denmark. He was married to fellow artist Gerda Wegener, who one day asked her husband to stand in for a female model who had failed to turn up.

The subsequent picture was so good that it led to a whole series of paintings (the public was subsequently somewhat shocked to learn that the beautiful woman they had all been admiring was in fact a man), with Einar adopting the name Lili Elbe. Gradually, he began to realise that he felt more at home as a woman than he did as a man and so began living full-time as a woman before becoming one of the first known people in the world to have a surgical sex change. He died at the age of forty-eight, after five largely experimental operations, the last being an attempt to transplant a uterus in order to allow him to become a mother. His body wouldn't accept it, though. The case at the time became something of a cause célèbre: the couple's marriage was annulled by the King of Denmark and she was even allowed to have the name Lili Elbe on her passport – Denmark, then as now, clearly being an extremely liberal country.

The novel, based on the story, had been an international sensation and plans to bring it to the screen had been on the cards for years. Directed by Tom Hooper – with whom Eddie had previously worked in *Les Mis* – with a screenplay by Lucinda Coxon, a number of major stars had been in the running to play Gerda, including Charlize Theron, Gwyneth Paltrow, Uma Thurman, Marion Cotillard and Rachel Weisz. The role ultimately went to Alicia Vikander. The reason why there was no similar list of male stars attached to the male lead is an intriguing one: it is believed that initially the role was going to be played by a woman. But minds were changed and so Eddie, of course, was Einar/Lili (with his slightly feminine looks he was a natural for the role), while other stars involved were Amber Heard, Matthias Schoenaerts and Ben Whishaw.

Anyone unfamiliar with the story must have been pretty startled when the first publicity shots were released in February 2015, shortly after the Oscars: Eddie appeared to have transmuted from a male professor confined to a wheelchair who could only communicate using a cheek muscle to a strikingly attractive brunette dressed in the high fashion of the 1920s and with a penchant for scarlet lipstick.

Just as had been the case for *The Theory of Everything*, Eddie did his research and started working with various people who could help to ease him into the role. He went to visit Lana Wachowski – the director of *The Matrix*, who is transgender – and worked with movement director Alexandra Reynolds to serve 'the minutiae of feminine physicality. We're looking at everything from a feminine perspective,' he told *Mail Online*. 'How to sit, to walk, to pose, roll on a pair of stockings. How to put on a pair of heels – and how to walk in them. Everything. The danger of surgery was so extreme [in the 1920s]. It's such a brave thing that Einar did. I think it's the most sensitive role I have played.'

Was this going to prove that Eddie could turn into almost anyone? Not since Daniel Day-Lewis (to whom Eddie had been compared, especially in Lewis's role as the artist Christy Brown: an Irishman born with cerebral palsy, who could only control his left foot) had any actor come across as so incredibly versatile. Or was it on the back of *The Theory of Everything* that these new roles were beginning to open up? 'I was actually offered *The Danish Girl* before Hawking,' he told *GQ*. 'People go, "Oh are you doing this transformative thing?" It's not a concerted choice. I think it will be a unique experience.'

It was certainly attracting a lot of attention and that was even before filming was complete. Pictures from the film began to emerge online, including a sequence in which, as Einar, he appeared to be getting beaten up by a couple of yobs and it wasn't long before Oscar speculation started there too. 'We just wrapped it exactly a week ago,' Eddie's co-star Matthias told *Collider* in May. 'Yeah, we were in Norway in a beautiful place on top of a mountain with a crazy panoramic view. I don't want to jinx it, but I can honestly say I'm pretty sure that Eddie Redmayne is gonna get his second Oscar nom, if not just the second Oscar period.'

It was certainly a possibility and the timing of the film could not have been more apt. Fascination with transgender issues was growing on both sides of the Atlantic: in the UK people had been initially stunned and then accepting when the boxing promoter Frank Maloney underwent a sex change to emerge as a woman called Kellie, while in the United States, the transformation of the Olympic sportsman Bruce Jenner into Caitlyn Jenner was almost daily making headline news. On television, a series called *Transparent*, in which a father called Mort Pfefferman, played by Jeffrey Tambor, informs his children that he now wishes to be known as Maura, was also wildly popular. Fashion was getting in on the act, with unisex clothing – known in Selfridge's department store as Agender – going mainstream. And the British edition of *Vogue* carried a feature headed 'Man, woman, neither, both,' which suggested that 'trans is having a moment'. If nothing else, *The Danish Girl* was certainly tapping into a trend.

Everyone wanted a piece of Eddie now and options were opening up for him like never before. Hollywood analyst Scott Feinberg pointed out that he could earn a fortune if he took part in a superhero movie: 'It is a big deal,' he said. 'Studios love enticing audiences by saying they have an Oscar winner on board. The next few weeks, months will be a very hectic, crazy time where a lot of offers will be made. Eddie has charmed everyone this year and Academy voters were very impressed by the physicality and commitment in his performance. Filmmakers want him for his likability and his talent.'

Eddie had previously expressed interest in doing a superhero movie (and that was certainly where the biggest money was, although he had also never given the impression of being in the business just for that) but what he actually did was sign up to voice the role of Ryan, a new engine character in the latest *Thomas the Tank Engine* movie, *Sodor's Legend of the Lost Treasure*. The character is 'overconfident and dismissive' and 'takes over for Thomas when Thomas is sent to work on another branch line'. 'I grew up loving to watch Thomas and his pals getting caught up in unexpected and mischievous adventures,' said Eddie. 'I jumped at the opportunity to get involved, and what fun it was.'

The film, expected to last sixty minutes, also boasted another very big name: Sir John Hurt, who played a character called Sailor John. 'Sailor John was something of a departure from what I usually do,' remarked Sir John with somewhat wry understatement, but he continued to say that he'd enjoyed himself as well. It was a minor but fun project that would either go straight to DVD or have a brief and limited release in the cinema.

Staying in child-friendly mode, next up was the announcement that Eddie, a big fan of *Harry Potter*, would be taking up the role of Newt Scamander in the forthcoming Potter spin-off *Fantastic Beasts and Where to Find Them*, which is meant to be one of the textbooks owned by Harry and authored by Newt. Warner Brothers' boss Greg Silverman said: 'Eddie Redmayne has emerged as one of today's most extraordinarily talented and acclaimed actors. We are thrilled to welcome him into J.K. Rowling's wizarding world, where we know he will deliver a remarkable performance as Newt Scamander, the central character in *Fantastic Beasts and Where to Find Them*.'

It was clearly something that Eddie was delighted about – he once said that he'd dreamed of playing a ginger-haired Weasley but hadn't made it through the auditions. And this too could be lucrative work: although Eddie is now estimated to be worth about £4 million, this is an insignificant amount in the world of Potter-money, where it is believed that Daniel Radcliffe has earned £95 million for his time in the role. The point was that he could make money from image rights, with his face plastered on to all manner of products such as lunch boxes and costumes. 'Eddie has his head screwed on when it comes to finances,' a source told *The Sun*. 'He knows how much money he could potentially make out of the new movie. Anything Harry Potter-related is hugely marketable and commercially lucrative.'

This could indeed be the start of a hugely lucrative new project. The film was based on J.K. Rowling's 2001 book of the same name, produced to raise money for Comic Relief, and the cover bore not her name but that of Newt Scamander. Warner Bros., which had produced the original *Harry Potter* films, had suggested Rowling basing a film upon the book and she agreed, deciding to write the screenplay herself. A trio of films was planned to be set in New York, seventy years before Harry's story began.

'It all started when Warner Bros. came to me with the

suggestion of turning *Fantastic Beasts and Where to Find Them* into a film,' J.K. Rowling said in a statement when the announcement was made. 'I thought it was a fun idea, but the idea of seeing Newt Scamander, the supposed author of *Fantastic Beasts*, realized by another writer was difficult. Having lived for so long in my fictional universe, I feel very protective of it and I already knew a lot about Newt. As hard-core *Harry Potter* fans will know, I liked him so much that I even married his grandson, Rolf, to one of my favourite characters from the *Harry Potter* series, Luna Lovegood.

'As I considered Warners' proposal, an idea took shape that I couldn't dislodge. That is how I ended up pitching my own idea for a film to Warner Bros. Although it will be set in the worldwide community of witches and wizards where I was so happy for seventeen years, *Fantastic Beasts and Where to Find Them* is neither a prequel nor a sequel to the *Harry Potter* series, but an extension of the wizarding world. The laws and customs of the hidden magical society will be familiar to anyone who has read the *Harry Potter* books or seen the films, but Newt's story will start in New York, seventy years before Harry's gets underway.'

It certainly was a role to get into and this is the story of his character: Newton Artemis Fido Scamander, to give him his full name, was born in 1897 and was himself a pupil at Hogwarts. His mother was a Hippogriff breeder and encouraged his interest in fabulous beasts – an interest that grew when he attended Hogwarts in Hufflepuff House. He then joined the Ministry of Magic in the Department for the Regulation and Control of Magical Creatures and, after many adventures, his contributions to Magizoology earned him an Order of Merlin, Second Class, in 1979.

Now retired, the story tells us that he lives in Dorset with his wife Porpentina and their pet Kneazles: Hoppy, Milly and Mauler. After Eddie's casting was announced, J.K. Rowling tweeted that she was 'thrilled'.

All in all, it is an extremely promising role in what looks set to be a lucrative franchise and, given how hugely different it is from anything he has done before, there is certainly no danger of Eddie getting typecast. What seems to be happening, though, decades before it usually does for anyone, is that Eddie appears to be turning into a national treasure. It is magic, no less.

CHAPTER FIFTEEN

EDDIE REDMAYNE, OBE

Halfway through 2015, Eton- and Cambridge-educated, award-winning and best-dressed actor Eddie Redmayne was awarded the OBE – Order of the British Empire – in recognition of his services for acting. (Benedict Cumberbatch got the slightly more senior CBE – Commander of the British Empire.) It was the culmination of what had been an astonishing year. Indeed, despite the amount of work he had built up and his wider exposure as a Burberry model, Eddie had in many ways been the acting world's best-kept secret. There was a sense that he had come out of nowhere, going from nought to ninety in a matter of seconds. Like so many of his fellow actors, he had been working for years to become an overnight success.

He has, though, proved himself to be one of the most

outstanding actors of a generation that is full of talent and his career looks set to soar. His range is astonishing and he has already shown that he can do everything from Greek drama to musicals via the portrayal of a brilliant mind trapped in a motionless body. And there is every indication that in the future he will, as many other actors before him have done, run a tandem career on stage and screen. Nonetheless, he remains modest about it all.

So what will he look for in the future? 'Trying to play something outside of what I've done before is definitely of interest,' he told *The Big Issue*. 'Whenever I read a script I can normally instantly have a gut reaction. It's an annoying phrase, "trust your instincts", because I'm like – okay, how do I know what that is? How do I define my instincts? Recognising what your instincts are is half the battle.'

But, according to Eddie, he has been given an insight into what is really important in life by virtue of his most famous role. 'I'm one of these people who gets caught up in the foibles and anxieties of my everyday bollocks, the small stuff,' he commented. 'Stephen was given this diagnosis of two years and says that beyond those two years, every day has been a gift. We all have limitations put on us in some shape or form by other people, it's how we supersede them that's interesting. Remembering we only have one shot is what I took away – to live each moment fully.'

Not that he's taking any of it for granted. The fear that afflicts most actors continues to afflict Eddie: 'Are you kidding me?' he said to *Interview* magazine when discussing whether he was calm about playing Stephen. 'I'm just one gigantic ball of rancid fear and self-consciousness. I'm entirely fueled by fear, so the fact that I knew it could be a catastrophic disaster made me unable to sleep, and made me work quite hard.'

In the event, of course, it was a sensational success. But there are plenty of challenges ahead. The marriage, while very happy, is still very new and any relationship encompasses challenges. But above all, Eddie will have to learn how to cope with his huge fame.

All actors want fame: they have to. It goes with the territory. You cannot be a big movie star if you are anonymous, but it can be very difficult to deal with being at the centre of attention of the entire world. For Eddie it has been building up slowly, allowing him to adjust gradually, and he also has the benefit of a big support network in the shape of friends and family. It was a momentous year, but it was also a stunning new beginning. A magnificent future lies ahead.

SELECTED CREDITS

2016
Fantastic Beasts and Where to Find Them
Role: Newt Scamander

2015
The Danish Girl
Role: Einar Wegener/Lili Elbe

Thomas & Friends: Sodor's Legend of the Lost Treasure
Role: Ryan (UK & US) (voice)

War Art with Eddie Redmayne (TV documentary)
Role: Himself

Jupiter Ascending
Role: Balem Abrasax

2014
The Theory of Everything
Stephen Hawking

2012
Les Misérables
Marius

Birdsong (TV mini-series)
Stephen Wraysford

2011–12
Richard II (stage)
King Richard II

2011
The Miraculous Year (TV movie)
Connor Lynn

My Week with Marilyn
Colin Clark

Hick
Eddie Kreezer

2010
The Pillars of the Earth (TV mini-series)
Jack

Red (stage)
Ken

Black Death
Osmund

2009
Glorious 39
Ralph

Powder Blue
Qwerty Doolittle

2008
Tess of the D'Urbervilles (TV mini-series)
Angel Clare

The Other Boleyn Girl
William Stafford

The Yellow Handkerchief
Gordy

Now or Later (stage)
John Jr.

2007
Elizabeth: The Golden Age
Thomas Babington

Savage Grace
Antony Baekeland

2006
The Good Shepherd
Edward Wilson Jr.

Like Minds
Alex Forbes

2005
Elizabeth I (TV mini-series)
Southampton

2004
Hecuba (stage)
Polydorus

The Goat, or Who Is Sylvia? (stage)
Billy

2003
Master Harold ... and the Boys (stage)
Master Harold

Doctors (TV series)
Episode: 'Crescendo'
Rob Huntley

2002
Twelfth Night (stage)
Viola

1998
Animal Ark (TV series)
Episode: 'Bunnies in the Bathroom'
John Hardy

1992–3
Oliver! (stage)
Workhouse boy no 46/Book boy

BIBLIOGRAPHY

Access Hollywood

Bloomberg News

British Theatre Guide

Bucks Free Press

Chicago Reader

Chicago Sun-Times

Curtainup.com

Daily Express

Daily Mail

Daily Star

The Daily Telegraph

Deadline.com

Digital Journal

Digital Spy

Empire magazine

Entertainment Spectrum
Esquire
Film4
Filmcritic.com
Fresh Air
The Hollywood Reporter
Intelligent Life
Interview magazine
London Theatre Guide
M magazine
National Catholic Register
New York Magazine
Newsweek
Ozus' World Movie Reviews
Quickflix
Radio Times
Rolling Stone
Screen Rant
Slant magazine
Sunday Express
The Sunday Telegraph
The Sunday Times
The Australian
The Globe and Mail
The Guardian
The *Huffington Post*
The Independent
The Independent on Sunday

The *Los Angeles Times*
The *Mirror*
The *National*
The *New York Observer*
The *New York Post*
The *New York Times*
The *New Yorker*
The *Observer*
The *Official London Theatre Guide*
The *San Francisco Chronicle*
The *Scotsman*
The *Stage*
The *Times*
The *Wall Street Journal*
Time Out
Toronto Star
USA Today
Variety
Village Voice
Vogue
The *Washington Post*
WhatsOnStage Review
Wired